QUICK
CROSSWORDS

THREE

Edited by Hugh Stephenson

First published in 2009 by Guardian Books,
Kings Place, 90 York Way, London N1 9GU

guardianbooks.co.uk

Guardian Books is an imprint of Guardian News and
Media Ltd.

Copyright © Guardian News and Media Ltd 2009

The moral right of Hugh Stephenson to be identified as the
editor of this work has been asserted in accordance with the
Copyright, Designs and Patents Act of 1988.

All rights reserved. No part of this publication may be
reproduced, stored in retrieval system, or transmitted in any
form or by any means, electronic, mechanical, photocopying,
recording, or otherwise, without the prior permission of both
the copyright owner and the above publisher of this book.

10 9 8 7 6 5

A CIP catalogue record for this book is available from the
British Library.

ISBN 978-0-85265-132-2

Printed and bound by CPI Group (UK) Ltd, Croydon, CRO 4YY

Design by Liz McCabe

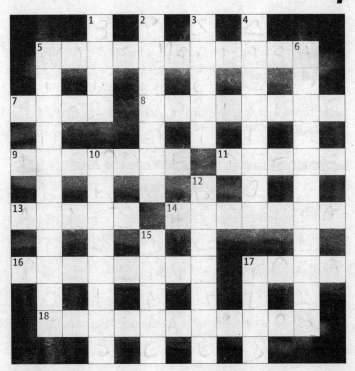

Across

5 Flooded dip in a road (5,6)
7 Stuck-up person (4)
8 Concerned with the sea (8)
9 Argue (7)
11 What's left in the bottle (5)
13 Girl's name (5)
14 Significance (7)
16 Keep — jam (8)
17 Something found on a coat, a bow and in the throat (4)
18 They will be prosecuted! (11)

Down

1 Fag end (4)
2 Support actively (with advertising?) (7)
3 Jolly good chap (though strikingly different from the parent!) (5)
4 Firm and unchallengeable (4-4)
5 Racing goal (7,4)
6 Of the same kind (11)
10 Journalists (8)
12 Death (7)
15 Cover with material (5)
17 Supply with eatables (4)

2

Across

5 State of being up to date (9)
8 Only — a lake (4)
9 Light for a second time (8)
10 Small creature (6)
11 On one's back (6)
13 Fragment (6)
15 Burlesque (6)
16 Word puzzle (8)
18 Loathe (4)
19 It lacks rhyme and metre (4,5)

Down

1 Desperate (8)
2 Private (6)
3 They take you down the board! (6)
4 Render insensible (4)
6 Strengthen (9)
7 Tryst with the unknown! (5,4)
12 Buy (8)
14 Rubbish — on which one is carried (6)
15 Parcel — mail boat (6)
17 Small boat's propellers (4)

Across

1 Trappings (13)
8 Important church (7)
9 Essential (5)
10 Face (4)
11 (Of voice) repeatedly rising and falling (4-4)
13 Competence (5)
14 Remain – bit of wood (5)
19 Division of the High Court of Justice (8)
21 Be acquainted with (4)
23 Emigré (5)
24 Old sailing ship (7)
25 Royal scholar (star of operetta and film) (7,6)

Down

1 Hair dressing (6)
2 Rifle (7)
3 Essential substance (4)
4 Insect (that eavesdrops?) (6)
5 Sail from A to B (8)
6 Release (3,2)
7 Assert (6)
12 Susan's injury? (5,3)
15 Eating place (7)
16 Means of entry (6)
17 Shining (6)
18 Slight pain (of conscience?) (6)
20 Farewell (5)
22 Libel (4)

4

Across

1 Bird of prey (11)
9 Term of endearment (5)
10 It makes the skin go pink and brown (7)
11 Salary (7)
12 Having lost colour (5)
13 Sordid (5)
15 Cut in two (like a stick?) (5)
20 Room on board (5)
22 Initially (2,5)
24 Glacial sediment (7)
25 Concede (5)
26 Splendid (11)

Down

2 Thoughtful (7)
3 Rolls's other half (5)
4 Legitimately positioned (6)
5 Difficult child (but can be grasped!) (7)
6 Hurt (5)
7 Egg beater (5)
8 Derogatory in an indirect way (5)
14 Allude to (7)
16 Workers' boss (7)
17 Rascal (5)
18 c/o (4,2)
19 Express (5)
21 Myanmar once (5)
23 Swiss currency unit (5)

5

Across

1 Colour (of a French cherry?) (6)
4 One dimension (6)
9 Watery fog? (3,4)
10 Monster with a woman's head (5)
11 End (5)
12 Determination (7)
13 Continuing from the old days (11)
18 First, second, third etc (7)
20 Bright light – latest news (5)
22 Thrown (5)
23 Witty saying (7)
24 Turn (6)
25 Against (6)

Down

1 Chess move (6)
2 Equip with better weapons (5)
3 Stiff and unnatural (7)
5 Characteristic spirit (5)
6 Great ape (7)
7 Tomboy (6)
8 Raconteur (or liar?) (11)
14 Defensive earthwork (7)
15 In an illegitimate position (7)
16 Money chest (6)
17 English river (6)
19 The dark (5)
21 Wall hanging – town in northern France (5)

6

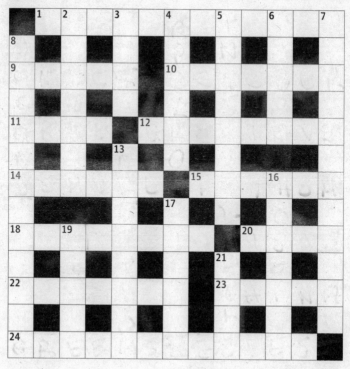

Across

1 Artistically irrational? (12)
9 Throw out (5)
10 Month (7)
11 Wind instrument (4)
12 "Happy and ___" (8)
14 Modest (6)
15 (Of depth) six feet (6)
18 Jamaican liqueur (3,5)
20 Egyptian goddess (4)
22 Slight suspicion (7)
23 Porcelain (5)
24 Elizabethan folk song (12)

Down

2 Regular – clothing (7)
3 Nonsense! (4)
4 Greek god (6)
5 Period between parts of a performance (8)
6 Forbidden (5)
7 When the three ships arrived! (9,3)
8 Alternative resource or plan (6,6)
13 The universe (8)
16 His cope (anag) (7)
17 Roman poet (6)
19 The greatest steeplechaser of all time, 1957-70 (5)
21 Land measure (4)

Across

1 School (not an exclusive one!) (13)
8 Eye – ball (3)
9 Scrap (5)
10 American author and poet, 1809-49 (3)
11 Top (5)
13 Employee (who can be civil!) (7)
15 Soft (6)
16 Ex-pupils (6)
19 Receptacle no longer seen in public places (7)
21 Up to (the point mentioned) (5)
22 Permit (3)
24 Melted together (5)
25 Animal (3)
26 One fifth (6,3,4)

Down

1 Used to get one through the hoops! (7,6)
2 Fairy queen (3)
3 Put aside (7)
4 Error – free thinking (6)
5 Rock bottom (5)
6 Small devil (3)
7 Illumination (8,5)
12 Old humorous magazine (5)
14 Steer for (3,2)
17 Wash clothes (7)
18 Plant with minty leaves used in herbal medicine (6)
20 Repair or re-equip machinery, ships etc (5)
23 Golfing accessory (3)
25 Change the colour (3)

8

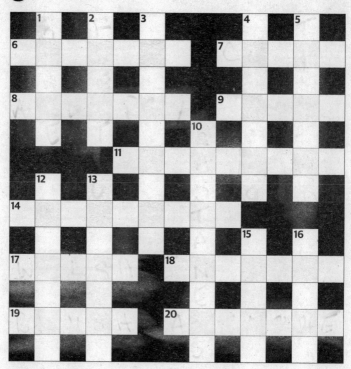

Across

6 Prepared to act (7)
7 Textile thread (5)
8 Damaging immune response to a substance (7)
9 Loose (5)
11 It decreases! (5,4)
14 Harm (2,5,2)
17 Celtic language (5)
18 Implore (7)
19 With high complexion (5)
20 Special member of an ambassador's staff (7)

Down

1 Holy Writ (5)
2 Swift – ships (5)
3 Dubbing (9)
4 One capable of wickedness (7)
5 Farm machine (7)
10 They accompany Spanish dancing (9)
12 Having some confidence (7)
13 Sit at the head of the table (7)
15 Painful noise (5)
16 Turning apparatus (5)

Across

1 Classical language (5)
4 Having the required ability (7)
8 Eggs (3)
9 Frame for drying clothes (5)
10 Proverbially sleepy rodents (7)
11 Larva of the daddy-long-legs (wearing trendy gear?) (13)
14 Scottish river (3)
16 Measured — recorded (5)
17 Dandy (3)
19 Civil defence officer (3-4,6)
21 Swollen (7)
23 A French dog (5)
24 Single (3)
25 Kind of well for Elsie, Lacie and Tillie (Lewis Carroll) (7)
26 Measure (more than a pint) (5)

Down

1 Flier (7)
2 Hoarse (7)
3 The NA in Nato (5,8)
4 Bounder (3)
5 Something necessary to the whole (4,3,6)
6 Edge (5)
7 Happening (5)
12 Speedy (5)
13 Self (3)
15 __ Baba (3)
17 One sharing short-lived enthusiasm (7)
18 Punishment (7)
19 Head monk (5)
20 French river (5)
22 Deer (3)

10

Across

1. Harmful (11)
9. Emasculate (5)
10. Show disapproval (3)
11. Be ill (3)
12. Lay into (7)
14. Captured (5)
15. Plating used as protective finish (6)
17. Lysander and Demetrius both loved her (6)
20. Kind of window — Oxford college (5)
22. Slaughter (7)
24. Sink (3)
25. Owing (3)
26. Least bright member of the class (5)
28. Where securities are traded (5,6)

Down

2. Odd (3)
3. Military government (5)
4. Discussion (6)
5. (Have a) quiet laugh (7)
6. Alas (5)
7. Inn (6,5)
8. English royal house (11)
13. Spoil (3)
16. Tuneful (7)
18. Extinct flightless bird (3)
19. Yell (6)
21. Bar of gold or silver (5)
23. System for detecting aircraft, ships and speeding motorists (5)
27. Born (3)

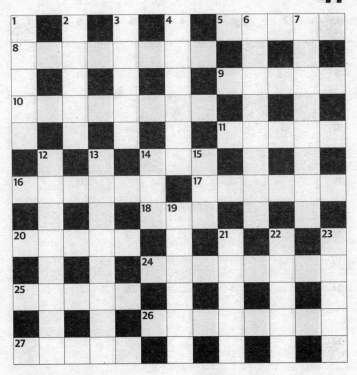

Across

5 Bring back (5)
8 Bitter tasting shrub (at the Scrubs?) (8)
9 Rob (5)
10 Of no value (8)
11 Error (5)
14 Cook – little fish (3)
16 Colour (to be born into!) (6)
17 Covered passage (6)
18 Tree (3)
20 Begin – jump (5)
24 It appears six days a week! (8)
25 Type of terrier (5)
26 Affable (8)
27 Type of artichoke (5)

Down

1 Weapon (5)
2 Inducement (5)
3 Suitor (5)
4 Dam (6)
6 Door – delight (8)
7 Mrs Mopp (8)
12 Country dance? (4,4)
13 Cut of pork (5,3)
14 Charge (3)
15 Sweet potato (3)
19 Paris gallery (6)
21 Building block (5)
22 Small (5)
23 Grind (5)

Across

1 Left at sea (4)
3 Wild emotion (8)
8 Put aside for a rainy day (4)
9 Type of spaniel (8)
11 Estimable (10)
15 Managed (3)
16 Subject (5)
17 Nothing (3)
18 Self-willed (10)
21 Midfielder (8)
23 Whirl (4)
24 Fit of 3 or 6? (8)
25 Present (4)

Down

1 Swap rods (anag) (8)
2 Cleric (8)
4 Sharp bark (3)
5 Threefold (10)
6 Anger (4)
7 ___-fairy (4)
10 Incessant talker (10)
12 Expected (5)
13 Detach (8)
14 Refinement (8)
19 Punish(ment) (4)
20 Confused impression (4)
22 Type of lettuce (3)

Across

6 Scottish estuary (5,2,5)

8 Importance (of the pound?) (6)

9 Receive (6)

10 Sports ground (7)

11 Open sore (5)

13 Pottery (from Vemeer's home town) (5)

15 Forebode (7)

17 Of small breadth (6)

19 Piercing with a horn (on Thames?) (6)

20 Beginning with the same letter or sound (12)

Down

1 Tear-jerking 1890s' Tin Pan Alley number (5,3,4)

2 Cold (6)

3 Firearm – type of wedding (7)

4 Old dyke builder (4)

5 Antifreeze (6)

7 Double of a living person (12)

12 Diver (7)

14 Hot (6)

16 17 at sea (6)

18 Seven days – a long time in politics! (4)

14

Across

1 Bulky (10)
7 Small stream (7)
8 Such a concern is not facing liquidation (5)
10 Roomy (4)
11 Pour too generously (8)
13 Venerate (6)
15 European capital (6)
17 Inventor of early photographic process, 1798-1851 (8)
18 Large jug (4)
21 Dodge (5)
22 Trim(ming) (7)
23 Old form of public transport (10)

Down

1 Very bright (5)
2 Flower – girl (4)
3 Reason (6)
4 West African (8)
5 The three classical dramatic principles of time, place and action (7)
6 It spanned a moat (10)
9 Forsyte author (10)
12 Breakfast dish (5,3)
14 Tramp (7)
16 Very sad (6)
19 Balance (5)
20 Accompanied solo song (4)

Across

1 Game bird (8)
5 Cut – bargain (4)
9 Milk container (5)
10 Attain (7)
11 Sussex cliffs (5,7)
13 Musical interval (6)
14 Absolutely correct (4,2)
17 Two melodies written or played together (12)
20 Provisional (7)
21 Irish lake (5)
22 Young woman (4)
23 (Of a court martial) improvised or summary (8)

Down

1 Burning point of candle – Scottish town (4)
2 Wealthy (7)
3 Greenhouse (12)
4 Upmarket (6)
6 22 who is related (5)
7 Agreeable (8)
8 A moving puzzle? (5,7)
12 Pathetic (8)
15 Style of haircut (7)
16 Basic textbook (6)
18 Say – complete (5)
19 Not barefoot (4)

16

Across

1 European language (5)
4 Post-1945 tension between the Soviet bloc and the West (4,3)
8 Tool (7)
9 Depression (5)
10 What the cock rules (5)
11 Toxophily (7)
12 Take a risk and have a go (6,4,3)
16 Garland for the head (of a small man?) (7)
18 Severe pain caused by wind (5)
20 Make straight (5)
21 Copy (7)
22 Visitor from elsewhere (7)
23 ___-panky (5)

Down

1 Relating to the stomach (7)
2 Muse of lyric poetry (5)
3 Relating to motion (7)
4 London road, centre of 1960s' fashion (7,6)
5 Reason (5)
6 Australian testing ground for nuclear weapons (7)
7 Very strange – card game (5)
13 Extraordinary (7)
14 Loutish (7)
15 Derision (7)
16 Ability to attract (5)
17 Girl's name (5)
19 Acquire knowledge (5)

Across

6 Woman's small private room (7)

7 Different (5)

8 Enhance the quality (of) (6)

9 Gentle and kind (this could be 9, reportedly) (6)

10 Mercy killing (10)

12 Childhood companion (10)

16 Loose a door fastener (6)

17 (Usually) chocolate-covered cream pastry (6)

18 Punishing (5)

19 Pyrenean state (7)

Down

1 European aristocrat (who can add?) (5)

2 Give counsel (6)

3 It runs though a town centre (4,6)

4 Verse (6)

5 Flightless bird (7)

9 Certainly! (2,3,5)

11 Overall – cover (7)

13 Small farmer of old (6)

14 Roll about (in mud or water) (6)

15 Record (5)

18

Across

1 Unauthorised use of another's property (6)
4 Swap – cane (6)
8 Move (5)
9 Back gate (7)
10 Freely (7)
11 Sequence (5)
12 French philosopher, 1596-1650 (9)
17 Nasal tone (5)
19 Knight of a crusading order founded in Jerusalem (7)
21 Cause of excessive anxiety (7)
22 Ordeal (5)
23 Printing mistakes (6)
24 Shoe (with a tongue?) (6)

Down

1 Small stone (6)
2 Sequoia (7)
3 Greek island (5)
5 Event that's rained off (7)
6 Tendency (5)
7 In need of food (6)
9 Financial officer (9)
13 Portion (7)
14 Silently bad-tempered (in one's tent?) (7)
15 Steady (6)
16 Screen (6)
18 Ire (5)
20 Driving force (5)

Across

5 Nursery rhyme couple (4,3,4)
7 Part of a tree (4)
8 Dickens's Nicholas (8)
9 Trip (7)
11 Nose (for tobacco?) (5)
13 Intoxicating (5)
14 "Money for ___" (3,4)
16 Pretender (8)
17 One of four gospellers (4)
18 Plant whose fruit is much used in jam and pies (5,6)

Down

1 Crust on wound (4)
2 With guile (7)
3 Decree (5)
4 Women's hatter (8)
5 Become a member (4,3,4)
6 Ramsay MacDonald was once its leader (6.5)
10 Song (8)
12 Discoloured in patches (7)
15 Tall and thin (5)
17 Encore! (4)

20

Across

5 Fruit and pastry dish (5,4)
8 Zn (4)
9 Well done! (4,4)
10 Part of the neck (6)
11 Most recent (6)
13 Jail (6)
15 Mutate (6)
16 Worker (8)
18 River of Tuscany (4)
19 Most fancied (9)

Down

1 Roomy (8)
2 Journey by air (6)
3 Saunter along (6)
4 Boast (about a bird?) (4)
6 Dangerous way to tread! (9)
7 Former naval recruiting service (5,4)
12 Social event of the 1773 season in Boston? (3,5)
14 Idea (6)
15 Poison traditionally used by South American Indians (6)
17 Wander about (4)

Across

1 Hurt deeply! (3,2,3,5)
8 Italian city, capital of Umbria (7)
9 Alter to suit (5)
10 Paradise (4)
11 Sudden rush (8)
13 Almanach de ___ (5)
14 Slit (5)
19 Tenant (8)
21 Girl's name (4)
23 Swap (5)
24 Difficult (7)
25 Accidents (13)

Down

1 PC – Cu (6)
2 Submarine weapon (7)
3 Wild party (4)
4 Fireplace (6)
5 Swamp (8)
6 Likeness (5)
7 Young animal (6)
12 Pastor (8)
15 Half man, half horse (7)
16 Drum played with the hands (3-3)
17 Betroth (6)
18 Bear-like animals (6)
20 Talons (5)
22 Take-off (4)

Across

1 Result (11)
9 Supple (5)
10 Allow to enjoy (7)
11 Kind of dolphin (7)
12 Origins (5)
13 Glide (like a fish?) (5)
15 Execute without trial (5)
20 Electric cable carrier (5)
22 Sticking out (7)
24 Explosive part of a missile (7)
25 Rude gesture (1-4)
26 Flat and uninteresting (11)

Down

2 Australia's hinterland and ... (7)
3 ... animals found there (5)
4 Infection of the throat (6)
5 Long in the tooth (7)
6 Musical instrument (5)
7 Wooden shoes (5)
8 Big meal (5)
14 Line touching circle (7)
16 English novelist, Wilkie, author of "The Woman in White" (7)
17 Produce offspring (5)
18 Look (at a goose?) (6)
19 Publish (5)
21 Big (5)
23 Hammer that lots come under! (5)

Across

1 Fairly – fair (6)
4 Cathedral and university city of northeast England (6)
9 Long plait (7)
10 Good (5)
11 Distances – areas (5)
12 Zero (7)
13 Depiction (11)
18 Gift – now (7)
20 Wireless (5)
22 Pull strongly (5)
23 Muddle (7)
24 Score (6)
25 Monty ___ (the snake!) (6)

Down

1 Spinach-eating sailor (6)
2 Keen (5)
3 Passage (7)
5 Not fulfilled (5)
6 Persistent attacker – hunting dog – bird of prey (7)
7 Defame (6)
8 Assault on one side (5,6)
14 Work (as a surgeon?) (7)
15 Despotism (7)
16 Consequence (6)
17 Control (6)
19 Throw out (5)
21 Money (for the baker?) (5)

24

Across

1 What's broken at Mach 1 (5,7)
9 Dramatist (5)
10 Wild horse (7)
11 Fever (4)
12 Sudden swirling movements (8)
14 Resound (6)
15 Wood (6)
18 London-Paris/Brussels express (8)
20 Sailing speed (4)
22 Germs (7)
23 Section of a long poem (5)
24 Done as a trial (12)

Down

2 Not well known (7)
3 Number (of the Muses?) (4)
4 Dickensian beadle (6)
5 Hold back (8)
6 Someone from Baghdad (5)
7 Recording (12)
8 Unpleasant (12)
13 American artist, 1834-1903, who painted his mother (8)
16 Situation giving rise to sudden good fortune (7)
17 Tranquilliser (6)
19 Sum up (abbr) (5)
21 Look over (4)

Across

1 Main London postal sorting office — Falkland Island airport (MPN) (5,8)
8 Pronoun (3)
9 Weight (5)
10 Participate in a winter sport (3)
11 Gas from oxygen — sea air! (5)
13 Small round boat (7)
15 Fold (6)
16 French author Marcel, 1871-1922 (6)
19 Crash land (on Shrove Tuesday?) (7)
21 West African country (5)
22 G&S princess (3)
24 Last event in a competition (5)
25 Hairstyle (3)
26 Anything goes! (2,5,6)

Down

1 Wrong idea (13)
2 Employ (3)
3 Naked from the waist up (7)
4 Float a boat (6)
5 Snake (5)
6 Fool (3)
7 No longer using a nappy (6-7)
12 Canoe (anag) (5)
14 Spanish enclave in Morocco (5)
17 Emblems of royalty (7)
18 Ball game (6)
20 Appalling (5)
23 Tree (3)
25 Ban (3)

26

Across

6 After second position (7)
7 Warm wrap (5)
8 Traditional spinster (3,4)
9 Stick – man (5)
11 One by one (9)
14 Florida resort (4,5)
17 Hold and use (5)
18 Part of the finger bone (7)
19 Office worker (5)
20 Swing (for flying?) (7)

Down

1 Cold (5)
2 Powerful card (5)
3 It measures height (9)
4 Walt, the poet (7)
5 Double (7)
10 One who fights for a wage (9)
12 Ice cream flavour (7)
13 Beg (7)
15 Range (5)
16 Fit panes of glass (5)

Across

1 Solemn promises (5)
4 Wise (7)
8 Dance (3)
9 Royal headdress (5)
10 Muslim veil (7)
11 European moth – legendary crone – rep hit Thomson (anag) (6,7)
14 Tell an untruth (3)
16 Wading bird (5)
17 South German city on the Danube (3)
19 Sudden illumination (though you still can't see) (8,5)
21 Diverge (anag) (7)
23 Exhibits – exhausts (5)
24 Poem (3)
25 Military formation (7)
26 Old magistrate (5)

Down

1 Best (7)
2 Kind of sandwich (7)
3 "Tell the truth and ____" (5,3,5)
4 Agent (3)
5 Evergreen climbing plant (7,6)
6 Irish nationalist, executed 1803 (5)
7 Symbol (5)
12 Dangerous woman (5)
13 Wise bird (3)
15 Unwell (3)
17 Increase in value (7)
18 French painter and sculptor, 1869-1954 (7)
19 Brass instrument (5)
20 Kind of coffee? (5)
22 Academic – river (3)

Across

1 Metal pan for cooking at table (7,4)
9 The Beatles' Eleanor (5)
10 People (3)
11 Expression of delight (3)
12 Rapid rise (7)
14 Scorch (a French monkey?) (5)
15 Aristocratic (6)
17 EU member state (6)
20 Move from one side to the other (5)
22 Girl's name (7)
24 Disorderly crowd (3)
25 Bed (3)
26 Railway line (5)
28 Where peals are cast? (4,7)

Down

2 Greedy beast (3)
3 Entrance hall (5)
4 Count (6)
5 Tang, for example (7)
6 Discoloration (5)
7 Annoying (11)
8 Knots used to shorten a rope (11)
13 Schoolmaster (3)
16 Rational (7)
18 Move fast (3)
19 Military show (6)
21 Permeate – inspire (5)
23 Giant (5)
27 Tune (3)

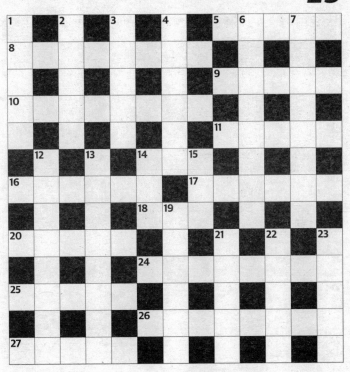

Across

5 Mass of bees (5)
8 Coxcomb (8)
9 Proverbially quiet creature (5)
10 Not hot (8)
11 Obiter dictum (5)
14 Prime number (3)
16 Where wild animals compete? (6)
17 Be added (6)
18 Very old ship (3)
20 Sharp (but not grave!) (5)
24 Authorised (8)
25 Hollow (5)
26 Small legless lizard (4-4)
27 Trap (5)

Down

1 Fruit (for the eye?) (5)
2 Projection (of Milligan?) (5)
3 Familiar (5)
4 Vegetable (6)
6 Seat for the Lord Speaker of the House of Lords (8)
7 What's left (8)
12 Hollander (who flies?) (8)
13 Troublemaker (8)
14 Hot drink (3)
15 Tree (3)
19 Lottery (6)
21 Opinions (5)
22 Wild ox (5)
23 Censure (5)

30

Across

1 It may be clenched (4)
3 Lazybones (8)
8 Small stream (4)
9 Panama, say (5,3)
11 It expels black liquid (10)
15 Jack – pitch (3)
16 (Make a) warbling sound (5)
17 Soviet space station (3)
18 Of a bird like the ostrich (10)
21 French person from close to the Italian border (or from Gilbert and Sullivan) (8)
23 Take care! (4)
24 Diplomatic (8)
25 In addition (4)

Down

1 Savageness (8)
2 Beneficial (8)
4 Plenty (3)
5 Abrasive material (5,5)
6 Pain (4)
7 Tax – obligation (4)
10 Railway worker (10)
12 Highland dance (5)
13 August – kind of beard (8)
14 Campaigns (8)
19 Accustomed (4)
20 American composer, 1974-1954 – American folk musician, 1909-95 (4)
22 Regret (3)

Across

6 Very small mammal (7,5)
8 Very small bit of clothing (6)
9 Expansion unlikely to last very long (6)
10 Insult (7)
11 Horse (5)
13 Wet ground (5)
15 Breakable (7)
17 Songbird (6)
19 Of the sea (6)
20 Selling price minus the cost of production (6,6)

Down

1 Symbol of cowardice (5,7)
2 Hole made by an explosion (6)
3 Main constituent of natural gas (7)
4 Attempt (with a dagger?) (4)
5 Marsupial (6)
7 Every cloud is said to have one (6,6)
12 Rails in the road (7)
14 Badly ventilated (6)
16 Housing for cars (6)
18 Majority tribe of Rwanda and Burundi (4)

Across

1 Add to (10)
7 Small, hardy chicken (from Livorno?) (7)
8 Test cricket ground (5)
10 Certain (4)
11 Height of ceiling etc (8)
13 Wrinkle (6)
15 Small carnivore (6)
17 Divinely prompted? (8)
18 Smart (4)
21 Following (5)
22 Nightclub entertainment (7)
23 Open area attached to a pub (4,6)

Down

1 Sweeten (5)
2 Water (on a billiard table?) (4)
3 Kind of finch (6)
4 Airs (8)
5 Apprehensive (7)
6 Sparks fly when you reach here (5,5)
9 Lack of complication (10)
12 Person who plans using drawings (8)
14 Waterfall (7)
16 Old kingdom of central England (6)
19 A Great Lake (5)
20 Not yet up (4)

Across

1 Helping hand for the family? (8)
5 Eager (4)
9 Loosen (5)
10 Condensation forming on the ground (7)
11 Given eternal fame (12)
13 Weed – shellfish (6)
14 English painter, noted for his sporting scenes, 1724-1806 (6)
17 Door that is not a door! (6,6)
20 Advanced position (7)
21 Blowing unevenly (5)
22 Unemployment pay (4)
23 Colonialist with a burden? (5,3)

Down

1 Standard (4)
2 Controversial work (7)
3 Person working for HM Revenue and Customs (3,9)
4 Staid (6)
6 Pot (found on the lawn?) (5)
7 Powder proverbially difficult to obtain (4,4)
8 Shakespeare play (7,5)
12 Place of execution (8)
15 Flower (7)
16 Short convulsive movement (6)
18 Praise (5)
19 Praise (4)

34

Across

1 Rugby forwards (5)
4 Supporter's badge (7)
8 Negative response (which may be point blank) (7)
9 Fear (5)
10 Basket for holding fish (5)
11 Mug (7)
12 None too soon! (3,6,4)
16 Dutch humanist, 1469-1536 (7)
18 Fasten(er) (5)
20 Submerge (5)
21 Being attended to (2,5)
22 Bombastic (7)
23 Herd of animals being driven (5)

Down

1 Old Turk (7)
2 Loot (5)
3 River (or wine?) (7)
4 Siren hospital (anag) (13)
5 Old carrying chair (5)
6 Wise men from the East (3,4)
7 Finished (5)
13 Cafe (3,4)
14 Thrilled (7)
15 Cost (7)
16 Finish (3,2)
17 Tropical fruit (5)
19 Where Davy Crockett died (5)

Across

5 Destructive ghost (11)

7 Jest (4)

8 Missile, sometimes verbal (8)

9 Snooper's aperture (7)

11 Put out (with a pinch?) (5)

13 Beautify (5)

14 They know things that are beyond reason! (7)

16 French Impressionist, 1830-1903 (8)

17 Facts (4)

18 Large and dangerous carnivore (7,4)

Down

1 Panic (in flight?) (4)

2 Burrowing desert rodents (7)

3 Once more (5)

4 Kitchen equipment (4,4)

5 Essential part of Christmas dinner (4,7)

6 Obsolete signalling device on cars (11)

10 Austerity (8)

12 Word with a more specific meaning – my phony (anag) (7)

15 Feed like sheep (5)

17 Beast(s) with horns (4)

Across

1 Robeson's Mississippi (3,3,5)
9 Prize (5)
10 Combatant (7)
11 Much revered and loved person (like Gandhi) (7)
12 Manner (5)
13 Stratagem (at cards?) (5)
15 Enlighten (5)
20 English diarist, 1633-1703 (5)
22 Spellbind (7)
24 Take (7)
25 Put off (5)
26 Fellow feeling between those with something in common (11)

Down

2 Hell for ___ (7)
3 In the middle of (poetic) (5)
4 Capital of the Bahamas (6)
5 Badly treated (3-4)
6 Girl's name (5)
7 Clement (but sounds mad!) (5)
8 Colour (5)
14 Dress (7)
16 Fashionable girl of the 1920s (7)
17 Bit of dust (5)
18 Napoleon's island saint (6)
19 Far from fresh (5)
21 Journal (5)
23 Load (5)

Across

1 Prescription (6)
4 Container (6)
9 Window covering (7)
10 Spirit (for the lamp?) (5)
11 Old English gold coin, first minted in 1351 (5)
12 Cheese (to be gorged?) (7)
13 Mansion fit for an 11? (7,4)
18 What still waters do, proverbially (3,4)
20 Greek letter (5)
22 Corn (5)
23 Convenience (7)
24 Outpouring of abuse (6)
25 Tension (6)

Down

1 Rebellion (6)
2 Particle (5)
3 One under the doctor (7)
5 Dispute (5)
6 Realm (7)
7 Not ours (6)
8 Kind of cactus (7,4)
14 North African port (7)
15 Topmost (7)
16 One side of the stage (6)
17 Indian fig tree (6)
19 Change (5)
21 Girl's name (5)

38

Across

1 German gutter (anag) – kitchen utensil (6,6)
9 Rash (5)
10 Collection of mail (7)
11 Box (4)
12 Despot (8)
14 Sewing implement (6)
15 Defeated (6)
18 Aesthetically pleasing (8)
20 By word of mouth (4)
22 The first of the three R's (7)
23 Evidence (5)
24 Proverbially, they make the most noise (5,7)

Down

2 Outmanoeuvre, theatrically (7)
3 Irish county (4)
4 Plaster of Paris (6)
5 Returned to previous condition or owner (8)
6 Old small drum (5)
7 Both sides (5,3,4)
8 It spread over Longfellow's village smithy (8,4)
13 Without being fully awake (8)
16 Confusion (7)
17 Enter as a thief (6)
19 Keen (5)
21 Musical work (4)

Across

1 Trappings (13)
8 Joint (3)
9 Boat (5)
10 Muscular spasm (3)
11 9s should keep off these! (5)
13 Lower the price (7)
15 Lie in wait for (6)
16 Lunatic (6)
19 City on the Tigris, destroyed 612 BC (7)
21 12 dance (5)
22 Frozen water (3)
24 Circumference (5)
25 Polish (3)
26 Army warrant officer (8,5)

Down

1 Very tough (2,4,2,5)
2 Go one better (3)
3 Roman name for Odysseus – book by James Joyce (7)
4 Ornate style (6)
5 Part of a bishop's 1 across (5)
6 Bolt's partner (3)
7 House of Lords, for example (6,7)
12 Top of the range cigar (5)
14 Solid geometric figure (5)
17 President Lincoln – Hebrew patriarch (7)
18 Israeli general and prime minister, 2001-6 (6)
20 Fashion (5)
23 Make a mistake (3)
25 British rule in India (3)

40

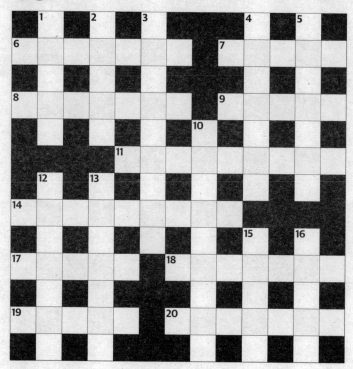

Across

6 Seclusion (7)
7 Admittance (5)
8 Uncloudiness (7)
9 Dress (5)
11 Trim and tidy (9)
14 Gilbert and Sullivan opera (9)
17 Precipitous (5)
18 It's not true (7)
19 Not tails! (5)
20 With speed (7)

Down

1 Amusing (5)
2 Piano key? (5)
3 Edible item (6,3)
4 State of lawlessness (7)
5 Maxim (7)
10 Revolting gladiator (9)
12 A sticky thing to be up! (3,4)
13 Extras (7)
15 The darkest colour (5)
16 Climb (5)

Across

1 Southern African (5)
4 Feeling confident (so heads down!) (5,2)
8 (Prefix indicating) new (3)
9 Mails (5)
10 Cheap time (for rail tickets, electricity etc) (3-4)
11 Eg – peg air mile tax (anag) (7,6)
14 Female animal (3)
16 Roman port (5)
17 Danger signal (3)
19 Young apprentice in the publishing trade (8,5)
21 Piece of furniture (7)
23 Planet (5)
24 Measure of printing type width (3)
25 Fee (7)
26 Unbending – back part of ship (5)

Down

1 Highest (7)
2 Unbending – strict (7)
3 Cannot be borne (13)
4 Excessively (3)
5 Ordinary clothes (8,5)
6 Brushed clean (5)
7 Genuine – excellent (5)
12 Bury (5)
13 Anger (3)
15 Conflict (3)
17 Daydream (7)
18 Marine mammal (7)
19 Accommodate (3,2)
20 Decorative pattern in furniture etc (5)
22 Although (3)

42

Across

1 Kind of warbler (11)
9 Entice (5)
10 Slippery customer? (3)
11 Vegetable (3)
12 Regard (7)
14 Team of experts (5)
15 Sailcloth (6)
17 Motor fuel (6)
20 Caribbean island – Scottish ben (5)
22 Spectrum (7)
24 Knock (3)
25 Part of play (3)
26 Not so many (5)
28 Office in a barracks (7,4)

Down

2 Pig meat (3)
3 Old church tax (5)
4 Agreement (6)
5 Backslide (7)
6 Poplar – Colorado ski resort (5)
7 Focus of disturbance (5,6)
8 They are not asked to dance (11)
13 Offspring (3)
16 Mollify (7)
18 Curved bone (3)
19 Harsh – beastly (6)
21 Snake (5)
23 Deduce (5)
27 TV doctor (3)

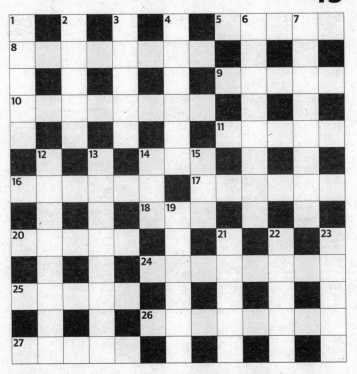

43

Across

5 Cram – material (5)
8 Water garden feature (4,4)
9 Shatter (5)
10 Souvenir (8)
11 Humorist (5)
14 Ancient (3)
16 Back of the neck (6)
17 Turn into bone (6)
18 Healthy (3)
20 Laughter (5)
24 Commendation (8)
25 Tilt (5)
26 Scowled (8)
27 Show to a seat (5)

Down

1 Be playfully provocative (5)
2 Depression (5)
3 Backbone (5)
4 Not 18 (6)
6 Eternal (8)
7 Proverbially, a prolific user of bad language (8)
12 He had a heel problem (8)
13 Manifold (8)
14 Away (3)
15 Small spot (3)
19 Transfix (6)
21 Go slowly (5)
22 Each (5)
23 Go effortlessly (5)

44

Across

1 Suspend (4)
3 Nobleman between earl and duke (8)
8 Bird (which can have fun?) (4)
9 Magnificent (8)
11 God-given? (6-4)
15 Instrument used in fishing (3)
16 Fastening (5)
17 Instrument used in gardening (3)
18 Later (10)
21 Tear (8)
23 Inform of a problem in advance (4)
24 Quarter of an old penny (8)
25 The Brontë nom de plume (4)

Down

1 Wait a minute! (4,4)
2 D-Day landing area (8)
4 Serpent (3)
5 Chessman (6,4)
6 Whirlpool (4)
7 Fizzy water (4)
10 From now on (10)
12 Flood (5)
13 Deficiency (8)
14 Private (8)
19 Treble or base? (4)
20 Mark of a wound (4)
22 Weight – style (3)

Across

6 Railway track (9,3)
8 Small pebbles (6)
9 Large marine reptile (6)
10 Bright red (7)
11 Complaining tone (5)
13 Brindled cat (5)
15 It's cheap at the price (7)
17 Obstinate (6)
19 Fault (6)
20 On and off (12)

Down

1 Sympathetic criticism (12)
2 Golf club (for the motorist?) (6)
3 One's business is road transport (7)
4 Optimum (4)
5 Key part of the human diet – stiffness of manner (6)
7 New Jersey coastal resort (8,4)
12 Authority to act (7)
14 Old chap (found down at the station?) (6)
16 With natural advantages (6)
18 Illuminating device (4)

46

Across

1 Emergency exit (4,6)
7 Relaxing ablution (3,4)
8 Metallic sound (5)
10 Liquid food (4)
11 Old presser (4,4)
13 Fertile (6)
15 Cut of beef (3-3)
17 Official mention of praiseworthy act (8)
18 (Clean with) absorbent pad (4)
21 The end (5)
22 Cut of beef (7)
23 Unfortunate (3-7)

Down

1 Causing 21 (5)
2 Highway (4)
3 Breathe out (6)
4 Mixed drink (8)
5 American plain (7)
6 Abashed (10)
9 Fizzy soft drink (6,4)
12 Bits of songs (8)
14 Rude shout at public meeting (7)
16 Shakespearean heroine (6)
19 Peculiar (5)
20 Stimulus (4)

Across

6 St Andrew's cross (7)
7 African striped animal (5)
8 Shakespeare's Weaver (6)
9 Select (6)
10 Meaning the same (10)
12 All-powerful (10)
16 The universe (6)
17 Oversensitive (6)
18 One (5)
19 Feign (7)

Down

1 Francis, English statesman d. 1626 – Irish painter d. 1992 (5)
2 Sets down in detail (6)
3 Colossal (10)
4 Improvement (6)
5 Abrupt (7)
9 Speculation (10)
11 Confiscate (7)
13 Occupant (6)
14 Reliable (6)
15 Move rolling stock – crash cars (5)

48

Across

1 Amuse verbally (6)
4 Terrible smell (6)
8 House traditionally provided for a Scottish Presbyterian minister (5)
9 One-time (7)
10 Drive mad (7)
11 Herb (5)
12 Varnished (9)
17 Indian monetary unit (5)
19 Something detached from the main body (7)
21 Stun (7)
22 With dignity (5)
23 Round figure (6)
24 Test (for illness, security etc) (6)

Down

1 Cure (6)
2 Ordinary – army officer (7)
3 Stay in bed (3,2)
5 Pig's foot (7)
6 Foolish person – sea bird – Enid Blyton character (5)
7 Estuary formed by the Trent and the Ouse (6)
9 Plaintive (9)
13 Mark with squares (7)
14 What babies and footballers do (7)
15 Dust-up (6)
16 Coloured pencil (6)
18 Nip (5)
20 Stimulant (5)

Across

1 The whole of the UK's capital city (7,6)
8 Bit of hair on the head (7)
9 Fattened chicken (5)
10 16 (4)
11 Look for – a view (8)
13 ___ de la Zouch, Leicestershire (5)
14 Large water bird (5)
19 Three score years and ten? (8)
21 Wound (4)
23 Town in east central Scotland (5)
24 Hero's lover, who drowned swimming the Hellespont to visit her (7)
25 Pi (informal) (13)

Down

1 Come together – understand (6)
2 Ruler or ruler's wife (7)
3 Container for liquid (used by the army?) (4)
4 Withdraw (6)
5 Happening (8)
6 Jacqueline, English cellist (2,3)
7 XC (6)
12 Remove from (8)
15 Unspecified (or annoying) person (2-3-2)
16 Invariably (6)
17 Token (6)
18 Refrain (6)
20 Criminal (5)
22 Farm building (4)

50

Across

1 Express the essentials succinctly – planet sauce (anag) (11)
9 Metal bolt (5)
10 Geometrical figure (7)
11 Girl's name (a moderate socialist?) (7)
12 Mistake (5)
13 Series that comes round (5)
15 Semi-divine female (5)
20 Due (5)
22 Completely out of date (7)
24 Roman Catholic priest's cap (7)
25 Frequently (5)
26 Outgrowth (11)

Down

2 Something new (7)
3 Thespian (5)
4 Cheap and nasty (6)
5 Random draw (7)
6 Big cat (5)
7 Kind of play (5)
8 Explosive sound through the nose (5)
14 Less heavy – barge (7)
16 Man-made material (7)
17 Kind of falcon – kind of horse! (5)
18 Pester (6)
19 Part of 7 (5)
21 Glasgow football stadium (5)
23 Boring job (5)

Across

1 Take up again (6)
4 The doubting Apostle (6)
9 Hurting (7)
10 Scottish poet (5)
11 Expand (5)
12 Very great (7)
13 Not exactly (11)
18 Chase (7)
20 Tower of many tongues (5)
22 Clear (5)
23 Gap (7)
24 Cooked long and slowly (6)
25 Road – Somerset home of Clarks, the shoemaker (6)

Down

1 Meal (6)
2 Point of a church (5)
3 Scarf (which reduces noise in the US?) (7)
5 Custom (employed when riding?) (5)
6 Metaphysical poet, 1621-78 (7)
7 Nurse (6)
8 Argument (11)
14 Wonder (7)
15 Overthrow (7)
16 ___ and pears (6)
17 Slander – insult (6)
19 Excessive (5)
21 Half of the happy couple (5)

52

Across

1 Kind of sofa (found in Derbyshire?) (12)
9 Pointer (perhaps a finger) (5)
10 Ray of natural light (7)
11 Dash (4)
12 Horse at stud (8)
14 Society magazine (6)
15 Desist! (4,2)
18 Treacle (8)
20 Insect (in your ear) (4)
22 Small lumps (of something precious) (7)
23 Imitative of a past style (5)
24 This state is on the way out (12)

Down

2 Water point (7)
3 Light blue (4)
4 Inferior substitute (6)
5 The end! (8)
6 Resin used in ointments and aromatherapy (5)
7 Person showing something off (12)
8 Light composition for chamber orchestra (12)
13 Cover for a marine mollusc (8)
16 Sensible and judicious (7)
17 Official count (6)
19 Nigerian city (5)
21 French cheese (4)

Across

1 Kind of preserve (10,3)
8 Keep on at — a horse (3)
9 Stand-in (5)
10 Silence (3)
11 Look at (the time?) (5)
13 Result of a quick 22 (7)
15 English composer, 1988-1973 (who lacked courage?) (6)
16 Girl's name (6)
19 Oxbridge "policeman" (7)
21 Glasgow's river (5)
22 Direct a weapon (3)
24 Spanish (or American) friend (5)
25 Primate (3)
26 Use all of my capacity (2,3,4,1,3)

Down

1 A walking advertisement? (8,5)
2 23 (3)
3 One who dodges an obligation (7)
4 Leak (6)
5 Cancel (a debt) — send (money) (5)
6 Dance (3)
7 Something that in fact did not happen (5-4-4)
12 Drier (5)
14 Name of eight kings of England (5)
17 Obverse of a strike (7)
18 Set fire to (6)
20 Early circumnavigator (5)
23 Not shiny — floor covering (3)
25 Part of a circumference (3)

54

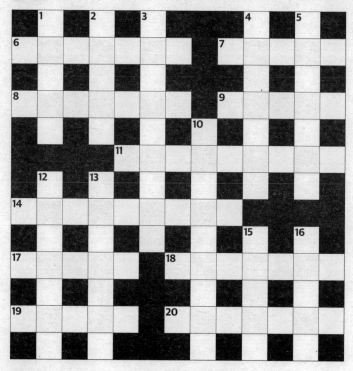

Across

6 Vocation (7)
7 Rush (5)
8 Mountaineer (7)
9 Rank (5)
11 Reasoning power (9)
14 U-turn (5-4)
17 Beast like a weasel (5)
18 Hair wash (7)
19 Icy rain (5)
20 Grazing land (7)

Down

1 Jump (underground?) (5)
2 Vertical line (5)
3 Compensate against loss (9)
4 Childish (7)
5 Make (7)
10 Footing established on a shore that's 12 (9)
12 Inimical (7)
13 Cooking vessel (7)
15 Flakes of soot – South African soldier and politician (5)
16 Fruit with a hard skin (5)

Across

1 Sightless (5)
4 Duck (7)
8 Australian bird (3)
9 Flowers (5)
10 Mauvish crimson (7)
11 Four-sided figure (13)
14 (Juvenile stage of) newt (3)
16 Senior clergyman (5)
17 Taxi (3)
19 National treasure house, established 1753 (7,6)
21 She writes in verse (7)
23 Dense (5)
24 Scottish county town and racecourse (3)
25 Held up (7)
26 Islamic republic, capital Sana'a (5)

Down

1 Flamboyant style (7)
2 Immediate (7)
3 Causing ruin (13)
4 Silent (but can be the word!) (3)
5 Manufacturing (but not heavy!) (5,8)
6 Al Capp's little cartoon character (5)
7 Speak with drawn-out vowel sounds (5)
12 Midday meal (5)
13 ___ Gardner, American actress, (1922-90) (3)
15 In favour of (3)
17 Chemical element, symbol Cs (7)
18 Unsophisticated person (7)
19 Two-legged creature (5)
20 Perfect (5)
22 Sorrowful (3)

56

Across

1 aka William Cody (7,4)
9 Hungarian wine (5)
10 Pigeon talk (3)
11 Cow talk (3)
12 Wrongdoer (7)
14 Group of people or animals (5)
15 Drink (6)
17 Family name of pioneer flying brothers (6)
20 Half man, half goat (5)
22 Performance (7)
24 Animal (with nine tails?) (3)
25 Period (3)
26 Creek (5)
28 Meaningful puff (5,6)

Down

2 Monmouth river (3)
3 Small handbill (5)
4 Place (6)
5 Absorbent pad (7)
6 Uncertain period of waiting – dance (5)
7 Creature resembling a twig (5,6)
8 Generosity to guests (11)
13 High shot at tennis (3)
16 Out of control with anger (7)
18 Obtain (3)
19 Chinese secret societies (6)
21 Object of spiritual significance (5)
23 Hang on (5)
27 Meadow (3)

Across

1 Garden flower (5)
4 Open by twisting (7)
8 Ancient Egyptian writing material (7)
9 Noble gas, symbol Rn (5)
10 It fits in a mortise (5)
11 Unplaced (7)
12 They look after people arriving (13)
16 Spread through everything (7)
18 Musical time (5)
20 Loud (5)
21 Renegade (7)
22 Army officer (7)
23 Wear away (5)

Down

1 Racing correspondent? (7)
2 Flower of the pea family (5)
3 Root vegetable (7)
4 Realistic – tunnel inmates (anag) (13)
5 Mouse-like animal (which can be tamed!) (5)
6 Compensation (7)
7 Draw back in pain (5)
13 Warm – drink (7)
14 Fertiliser (7)
15 Whip – cause of great suffering (7)
16 Extreme fear (5)
17 Indo-European (5)
19 Saying (5)

58

Across

6 Metal link (7)
7 Back tooth (5)
8 Bring in – meaning (6)
9 Produce piglets (6)
10 Printed matter (10)
12 Concerned with the correct way of doing things (10)
16 Tension (6)
17 Fine point (6)
18 Iraqi city (5)
19 Protection (7)

Down

1 Piece of verse? (5)
2 Place for teaching (porpoises?) (6)
3 Trite remarks (10)
4 Belgium's most famous detective! (6)
5 Not sweet (7)
9 Harbinger (10)
11 Woodworker's tool (7)
13 Fruit (6)
14 Small case hung round the neck (6)
15 Pile of hay (5)

Across

1 Native American tent (6)
4 Plug for a beer barrel – tap for an American (6)
8 Intuitive skill (5)
9 Colossal (7)
10 Found out – sounded like thunder (7)
11 Upstairs room (5)
12 Unattractive (9)
17 One who drinks too much (5)
19 Sign of trouble? (7)
21 Bewilder (7)
22 Well-off Russian peasant (5)
23 Lay bare (6)
24 Entreaty (6)

Down

1 Light biscuits (6)
2 Structure of language (7)
3 The cruelest month (5)
5 Kind of stamp (7)
6 Gleam (5)
7 Dug channel (6)
9 Former English county, which still has a cricket team (9)
13 Thisbe's lover (7)
14 Altogether (7)
15 Suffocate (6)
16 Nicotine addict (6)
18 Stoutish (5)
20 Creator (5)

60

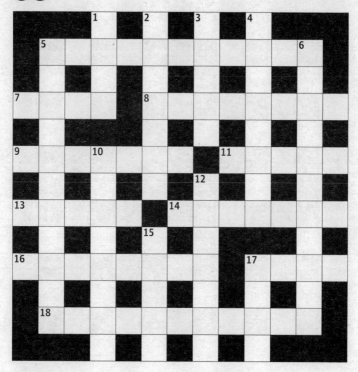

Across

5 John Buchan novel (with coloured covers?) (11)
7 Schoolmaster – magistrate (4)
8 At 12,500 ft, the highest lake in the world (8)
9 Each of different forms of a radioactive element with the same number of protons (7)
11 Talk (like a whale?) (5)
13 Ghost – spy (5)
14 Disappointment (7)
16 Mexican hat (8)
17 Highlands valley (4)
18 Informal (4,3,4)

Down

1 Kiss and cuddle – part of the body (4)
2 Parts of the foot (7)
3 Its capital is Port-au-Prince (5)
4 Proverbially, it bleeds profusely (5,3)
5 Impermeable to oil or fat (11)
6 Solely (11)
10 Anxious (8)
12 Parts of a ship's rigging (found in graves?) (7)
15 Started (5)
17 Smash and ___ (4)

Across

5 Old wheeled conveyance for invalids (4,5)

8 Playwright, Robert, 1924-95 (4)

9 Charon's function at the River Styx (8)

10 Being (6)

11 Loose threads – makes a continuous rhythmic sound (6)

13 Like a dog in a long, pointless story? (6)

15 Pool (connected to duck in the story) (6)

16 Involved as a necessary part (8)

18 Surrender (4)

19 History of events (9)

Down

1 Dancing (like Matilda?) (8)

2 Evasive (6)

3 Desire for drink (6)

4 Compassion (4)

6 Illegal liquor (drunk at night?) (9)

7 Breakfast preserve (9)

12 Mockery (8)

14 Coward's colour (6)

15 English of a kind! (6)

17 Old Turkish military commander (4)

62

Across

1 Dismay (13)
8 Ruler exercising a sovereign's authority (7)
9 Secretory organ (5)
10 Civil disturbance (4)
11 Facial hair (8)
13 What little children should not be! (5)
14 Nullify legally (5)
19 Whisky and soda with ice in a tall glass (8)
21 Circular collapsible tent (4)
23 Weapon of mass destruction (1-4)
24 Thin sheet with letters and patterns cut out (7)
25 Good luck (said to air travellers?) (5,8)

Down

1 Large dark place (where the Beatles were born?) (6)
2 Phrase signifying approval (4,3)
3 Someone from Istanbul? (4)
4 Swing (6)
5 Roman emperor (8)
6 Stupid (5)
7 Person altogether in the altogether (6)
12 Very likely (8)
15 Very small quantity (7)
16 Cover (6)
17 Liquid part of blood (6)
18 Ancient writing instrument for wax tablets (6)
20 Collection (5)
22 Unwanted plant (4)

Across

1 Brittle yellow-brown sweet (12)

9 Author of fables (5)

10 Almost but not completely as described — computer generated (7)

11 Period spent boxing (or drinking?) (4)

12 Bully verbally (8)

14 Conundrum (6)

15 Ostentatious (6)

18 Burial ground (8)

20 Otherwise (4)

22 Past its usefulness? (7)

23 Style of classic Greek architecture (5)

24 Very secure (like the Bank of England?) (4,2,6)

Down

2 Heretical (7)

3 Record (found at the end of the race?) (4)

4 Return to type (6)

5 English county (8)

6 Ceasefire (5)

7 "Speak now or for ever ____" (4,3,5)

8 Where to go to see a fair lady on a white horse (7,5)

13 Excess (8)

16 Be quiet! (7)

17 Crucial point for decision (regarding credit?) (6)

19 Theme (5)

21 Place — stead (4)

64

Across

1 Of many shapes and colours (13)
8 Help (3)
9 Northeast African country (5)
10 Become more solid (3)
11 Sign up (5)
13 Hertfordshire town – no story (anag) (7)
15 What is to come (6)
16 African antelope (6)
19 Moral (7)
21 Nose drip (5)
22 Deep groove (3)
24 Smith's block (5)
25 Trap – drink (3)
26 Area of West London (9,4)

Down

1 The tart stealer (5,2,6)
2 Boy (3)
3 Parochial? (7)
4 Refuse (6)
5 Careful, like a Scotsman (5)
6 Its used for hanging things from (3)
7 There are twelve of them (8,5)
12 Vomit (5)
14 Make fun of (5)
17 Small round balls that are a bad thing to lose (7)
18 Pasture plant (6)
20 Come together violently (5)
23 Digit (3)
25 Large dark antelope (3)

Across

6 Behave servilely – kind of bed (7)
7 Worth little (5)
8 Deadlock (7)
9 Rap (5)
11 Worth more than money can buy (9)
14 Military formation (4,5)
17 Sign of the zodiac (5)
18 Intellectual (like Humpty-Dumpty?) (7)
19 Runny (5)
20 Defensive structure (7)

Down

1 Basic structure – incriminate by false evidence (5)
2 Bit (of a fight?) (5)
3 Part of school building (9)
4 Wooden tile (found on the beach?) (7)
5 Dead body (7)
10 One made to carry the can (9)
12 Thing (in a newspaper?) (7)
13 Not the kind of victory one would wish for (7)
15 Geometric figure (5)
16 Chivvy – boy (5)

66

Across

1 Under (5)
4 Beetroot soup (7)
8 Marriage response (1,2)
9 Undisputed heavy-weight champion of the world, 1987 (5)
10 Not likely to cause disagreement (7)
11 In great style (13)
14 Ocean (3)
16 What a vice does (5)
17 Catch — arrest (3)
19 Working at home (5,3,5)
21 Unemployable (7)
23 Monies advanced (5)
24 In the style of (1,2)
25 Pantomime widow (7)
26 Tall grass (5)

Down

1 Before the expected hour (7)
2 Italian dish (7)
3 Successful run (in the nude?) (7,6)
4 Long evening stole (3)
5 One of a group of Oxford students from abroad (6,7)
6 Vault beneath a church (5)
7 Very small (5)
12 Erse (5)
13 Old card game — lavatory (3)
15 Recede (3)
17 Bottle (7)
18 Makes happy (7)
19 Grown-up (5)
20 Greek letter (5)
22 Utter — for example (3)

Across

5 Star Trek's half-Vulcan – American paediatrician (5)
8 The United States (5,3)
9 Kind of newspaper (5)
10 Restrain (4,4)
11 Fixed period of work (5)
14 Fuss (3)
16 For nothing (6)
17 Obstruct (6)
18 Edge (3)
20 Intuitive guess (5)
24 Playful (8)
25 Cut wool (5)
26 One is owed money (8)
27 Austrian state, capital Innsbruck (5)

Down

1 Japanese dish (5)
2 Hurt with hot water (5)
3 Classic flat race (5)
4 (Of oily foods) tasting or smelling bad (6)
6 School period without lessons (8)
7 Draining utensil (8)
12 Subject to air currents (8)
13 Short and sharp (8)
14 Fire residue (3)
15 Unit of electrical resistance (3)
19 Dominion over other lands (6)
21 One easily shocked (5)
22 Half century (5)
23 Facial hair (5)

68

Across

1 Wild animal (could be lone!) (4)
3 Top of the bill (4,4)
8 Not one (4)
9 Memento (8)
11 Sycophantic (10)
14 Forte (6)
15 Mary's sister (6)
17 Modulation (10)
20 Means of influencing a result (8)
21 Move slightly (4)
22 Strength (8)
23 English composer, d. 1623 – American explorer, d. 1957 (4)

Down

1 Unexpected gain (8)
2 Swedish founder of modern systematic biology, 1707-78 (8)
4 Supposition (6)
5 Contrition (10)
6 US state, capital Salt Lake City (4)
7 Want (4)
10 Critical siege and battle in WWII (10)
12 With precision (8)
13 (Of style) artificial (8)
16 Pledge – difficult situation (6)
18 Oh dear! (4)
19 Test cricket ground (4)

Across

1 Where plants and garden tools are kept (7,4)
9 Make less refined (9)
10 Absolute principle in Chinese philosophy (3)
11 Indian 17 (5)
13 Holds in high regard (7)
14 Repeat performance (6)
15 Mood – wit (6)
18 More circular (7)
20 System of belief (5)
21 Negative (3)
22 Weighty (9)
24 American pit viper (11)

Down

2 Lubricate (3)
3 Instructor (7)
4 Fastened – caught – exposed (6)
5 Covering (5)
6 Kind of steak (9)
7 Imperious (11)
8 Plant with pungent root (11)
12 Girl's name (9)
16 Dirty (7)
17 Queen's son (6)
19 Base establishment (5)
23 Obnoxious person (3)

70

Across

6 Unofficially (3,3,6)
8 Greatest (6)
9 Loathe (6)
10 Seen – tarnished (7)
11 Cereal crop (5)
13 Look threatening (5)
15 Die down (7)
17 Once more (6)
19 Ancient Greek sanctuary, seat of the Oracle (6)
20 A Jezebel? (7,5)

Down

1 Musical – ocean (5,7)
2 Waterborne (6)
3 Idle talk (7)
4 Network (4)
5 Put an end to (6)
7 Get up! (4,3,5)
12 End of the day (7)
14 Light passenger boat – large barge (6)
16 Dancer who wanted John the Baptist's head on a plate (6)
18 Take notice of (4)

Across

1 Kind of cross-country run (10)
7 No novice (3,4)
8 Hereditary prince of Hyderabad (5)
10 Idiot (4)
11 Weigh down (8)
13 Milky alcoholic drink (3-3)
15 City, province and lake of northwest Italy (6)
17 Author of "The Water-Babies" (8)
18 Object of adoration (4)
21 Proverbially thick-skinned animal (abbr) (5)
22 Help for those in need (7)
23 Done without thought (as by a machine?) (10)

Down

1 Lever on a bicycle or piano (5)
2 Traditional Irish fuel (4)
3 Gnawing animal (6)
4 Central American country, capital Tegucigalpa (8)
5 Large (7)
6 Bird that can 19 (10)
9 Star music hall singer, 1870-1922 (5,5)
12 Indeed (archaic) (8)
14 Discharge of artillery (7)
16 Guiding light (6)
19 (Military) exercise (5)
20 French chalk (4)

Across

6 Storehouse (7)
7 Substance creating reefs (5)
8 Fated to perish (6)
9 Get (6)
10 Lawful (10)
12 Hotel worker (4,6)
16 Belgian city (6)
17 Cause to be liked (6)
18 Violence (5)
19 Land area (7)

Down

1 Before (5)
2 Creature (6)
3 Enormous (10)
4 Nethermost (6)
5 The spice of life? (7)
9 Extend (10)
11 Soldier (7)
13 It's what's left (6)
14 Steering device (6)
15 Author of "Brideshead Revisited" (5)

Across

1 Ornamental band (6)
4 Sharp tasting (beer?) (6)
8 Thigh bone (5)
9 Create an effect (7)
10 Glowing (7)
11 Following (5)
12 The Walrus's companion (9)
17 Was unwell (5)
19 Can be heard (7)
21 Ate — drank (7)
22 Swedish-born American actress, who "wanted to be alone" (5)
23 French South Pacific island (6)
24 Ships regularly drop one (6)

Down

1 Not 11 (6)
2 Wandering (7)
3 Immature insect form (5)
5 Place within (7)
6 Give medical attention (5)
7 Holiday destination (6)
9 Uninformed (2,3,4)
13 Old soldier (7)
14 Renewal (7)
15 Floor covering (6)
16 Diversion (6)
18 Sudden movement (5)
20 Entrench (3,2)

74

Across

5 Anti-submarine weapon (5,6)
7 A piece of cake! (4)
8 Rabble (4-4)
9 Family (7)
11 To be expected (5)
13 Ornamental stone (5)
14 Fundamental principles on which something is based (7)
16 Medical institution (8)
17 Keen (4)
18 Professional misconduct (11)

Down

1 Lively for one's age (4)
2 Name of two English kings (7)
3 Slight smell (5)
4 Pipe to which a fire hose can be attached (3,5)
5 Parlour (7,4)
6 Give the vote to (11)
10 Subtropical fruit tree (4,4)
12 Turn aside (7)
15 Tempest (5)
17 Sharp (4)

Across

5 Universal (9)
8 Manage (4)
9 Free promotional item – inadvertent revelation (8)
10 Soviet leader during WWII (6)
11 Mourn (6)
13 Cultural commentator (6)
15 Not serious (6)
16 Rider's foot supports (8)
18 Lose colour (4)
19 Certainly (9)

Down

1 Bedspread (8)
2 Large drink container (6)
3 Turn on an axis (6)
4 Notion (4)
6 Future generations (9)
7 Old artillery attack (9)
12 Tie up (a boat) (4,4)
14 Plump (6)
15 Bump (6)
17 Bird (that cheats?) (4)

Across

1 Relish – difficult situation (6)
4 Strike repeatedly – meal where one helps oneself (6)
9 Person under instruction (7)
10 Weapon (5)
11 Central African river (5)
12 John Gilpin was one "of credit and renown" (7)
13 Robert the Bruce's victory over the English in 1314 (11)
18 Something lacking substance (7)
20 Playing cards used in fortune-telling (5)
22 Show reluctance (5)
23 Show off (7)
24 Add condiments (6)
25 Decorative extras (6)

Down

1 Coup d'etat (6)
2 Link together (5)
3 English cathedral city – US president (7)
5 Disconcert (5)
6 Cold storage (7)
7 Cruel ruler (6)
8 Vagrant living by the seaside? (11)
14 Condition of the blood (7)
15 Cut to pieces (7)
16 Card suit (6)
17 Prestige (6)
19 Trunk (5)
21 Rise up (5)

Across

1 Rationally inexplicable event (5)
4 The weed (7)
8 Yoko __ (3)
9 Eating iron (5)
10 Very cold – very slow (7)
11 Had responsibility for (13)
14 The First Lady (3)
16 Push gently (5)
17 Fizzy drink (3)
19 Take into account (4,9)
21 More daft (7)
23 Sporting event(s) (5)
24 World Wide Web address (3)
25 Red pepper powder (7)
26 Leftovers (5)

Down

1 (Of a performance) essential to go to (4-3)
2 Enthusiastic follower (7)
3 Argumentative meeting between two parties (13)
4 Measure of the insulating quality of clothes etc (3)
5 Aldous Huxley novel (5,3,5)
6 Wept (5)
7 Looked lasciviously (5)
12 Knob-shaped (5)
13 Italian novelist, Umberto (3)
15 By way of (3)
17 Flamboyant confidence (7)
18 Squeezes together (7)
19 Vocal and/or instrumental sounds (5)
20 Australian folk hero, Ned (5)
22 Herbal shrub (3)

Across

1 Newspaper feature (by an aunt?) (5,6)
9 Dutch painter (9)
10 Greek letter – Basque separatist movement (3)
11 Material (5)
13 Device used to improve room air quality (7)
14 Nervously (6)
15 Ancient Greek city on the site of modern Izmir in Turkey (6)
18 Caretaker (7)
20 French river – WWI battle (5)
21 Trigonometrical function (abbr) (3)
22 Oz (9)
24 Suggested scheme (11)

Down

2 Part of the mouth (3)
3 Arctic creature with a long tusk (7)
4 Frank (6)
5 Allow through the door (3,2)
6 Turmoil – whirlpool (9)
7 Exceptionally good (11)
8 Road for vehicles (11)
12 Person in charge of an event (9)
16 Semi-aquatic North American rodent (7)
17 Time of great difficulty (6)
19 Gentleman of the road (5)
23 Sign of the zodiac (3)

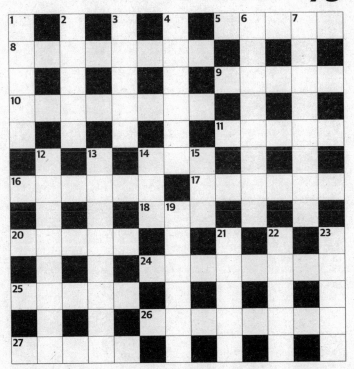

Across

5 Disgrace (5)
8 Round – kind of letter (8)
9 Length of wood (5)
10 Male sexual organ (8)
11 One of a flight (5)
14 Choose (3)
16 Professional Japanese hostess (6)
17 Ornamental alloy (6)
18 Tear (3)
20 Fish-eating mammal (5)
24 Awkward to handle (8)
25 Denude (5)
26 Difference between value of imports and exports (5,3)
27 Ugly Scandinavian giant (or dwarf) (5)

Down

1 He died in 1912 returning from the South Pole (5)
2 Crowd (5)
3 Shockingly sensational (5)
4 Polling organisation (6)
6 Sporting interval (4-4)
7 Spanish lace scarf (8)
12 One who has a will (8)
13 Very particular (8)
14 Blade (3)
15 Spinning toy (3)
19 Disregard (6)
21 Following a twisting course (5)
22 Personal websites (5)
23 Imaginary figure – slender woman (5)

Across

1 Infant (4)
3 Sapper's private detective, Bulldog ___ (8)
8 Yield (4)
9 Mishap (8)
11 Very low velocity! (6,4)
14 Parts of the foot (6)
15 Parent (6)
17 Sent to Coventry (10)
20 Bucolic (8)
21 Short animal tail (4)
22 Terrible (8)
23 Walk like a policeman? (4)

Down

1 No place for a driver! (4,4)
2 Ability to keep afloat (8)
4 Write out again (6)
5 Opportunity for self-enrichment (4,6)
6 Frank (4)
7 Appointment (4)
10 Mountaineering aid (10)
12 Relating to the body (8)
13 Came before in point of time (8)
16 Decree (6)
18 Mimics (4)
19 European capital (4)

Across

6 Mutually incompatible – a Hittite clan (anag) (12)

8 He was converted on the road to Damascus (2,4)

9 Change into a chrysalis (6)

10 Personal property (7)

11 Produce offspring (5)

13 Humorous imitation of something (5)

15 Seriousness (7)

17 Writing implement (6)

19 Action programme (6)

20 Sea food? (5,7)

Down

1 Word considered in grammatical terms (4,2,6)

2 Odourless flammable gas (6)

3 Sports person (7)

4 Profound (4)

5 Cured fish (6)

7 Genuine quality (12)

12 Suggest (7)

14 Take (6)

16 Bravery (6)

18 Part of the ear (4)

Across

1 Parallel to the ground (10)
7 Such sweet sorrow? (7)
8 Hale and hearty — deception (5)
10 Totter (4)
11 The green-eyed monster (8)
13 Tropical bird with large bill (6)
15 Not working! (2,4)
17 Artist's material (3,5)
18 From Bangkok (4)
21 Perverted person (slang) (5)
22 Falsehood (7)
23 Generally (2,3,5)

Down

1 Domesticated herbivore (5)
2 Destruction (4)
3 Capital of Croatia (6)
4 Aristocracy (8)
5 Normal (2,5)
6 Alcoholic (10)
9 Financially untrustworthy (3-2-5)
12 Light biscuit with almonds (8)
14 Not fortunate (7)
16 Display (6)
19 Residence (5)
20 Leading light (4)

Across

1 Orchestral instrument (8)
5 Part of the leg (4)
9 Foreign (5)
10 Jumbled mess (7)
11 Former political organisation led by Gladstone (7,5)
13 Glory (6)
14 Tree (6)
17 Dark liqueur (6,6)
20 French castle (7)
21 Freeze (3,2)
22 Completes (4)
23 Poet who wrote "The Charge of the Light Brigade" (8)

Down

1 Cover – shawl (4)
2 Point of view (7)
3 Person who achieves the impossible? (6-6)
4 Divine drink (6)
6 Change (5)
7 Number – to fry wot? (anag) (5-3)
8 Entreaty (12)
12 Vehicle (8)
15 They partner snakes! (7)
16 Slow in the uptake (6)
18 Antelope (5)
19 On top of (4)

84

Across

1 Tramp (4)
3 Stubborn (8)
9 Meat, spices and breadcrumbs fried together (7)
10 Ruing (anag) (5)
11 Forward thrust (5)
12 Fungal timber decay (3,3)
14 Beyond which one will not go (8,5)
17 Ordinal number (6)
19 Tree (5)
22 Assumed identity (5)
23 One from Kabul? (7)
24 Liquids used to dissolve other substances (8)
25 Carve on a surface (4)

Down

1 Innocuous (8)
2 Mixing vessel (5)
4 Excessively compassionate person (8,5)
5 Excessively expensive lending (5)
6 (Of reasoning) based on theory not observation (1,6)
7 Nervous (4)
8 One hundredth of a rouble (6)
13 Marine creature (8)
15 First (7)
16 Promise (6)
18 Rush (5)
20 Early version of a document (5)
21 Facial features (4)

Across

6 Rare metal – I'm Nehru (anag) (7)
7 Spacious (5)
8 Subject to death (6)
9 Piece of photographic equipment (6)
10 Token payment (10)
12 Visually attractive quality (10)
16 Piece of farm equipment (6)
17 Conditional release from prison (6)
18 Scottish name (for a cow?) (5)
19 Breathe in (7)

Down

1 Fire! (5)
2 Grab (6)
3 Exotic (10)
4 Kind of window (6)
5 Loving (7)
9 Write letters (10)
11 The Emerald Isle (7)
13 Sign of the zodiac (6)
14 Line of colour (6)
15 Speak out without thinking (5)

86

Across

1 Bemuse (with drink?) (6)
4 Not confirmed – temporary (6)
8 Dead easy! (5)
9 21 to Thursday (7)
10 Middle Eastern country (7)
11 Afterwards (5)
12 Root out completely (9)
17 Czech novelist, author of "The Trial" (5)
19 Go off at a tangent (7)
21 Sea duty (anag) (7)
22 Racoon-like animal with snout and ringed tail (5)
23 Buy back (6)
24 Secret (6)

Down

1 Too simple (6)
2 Maim (7)
3 Buy supplies (of) (3,2)
5 It softens the sound of a C (7)
6 Clumsy (5)
7 Miniature racing car (2-4)
9 Robinson Crusoe's companion (3,6)
13 Nonsense! (7)
14 Raise (7)
15 He's on ice! (6)
16 Casual dress (1-5)
18 Area (5)
20 Lizard (5)

Across

1 Custom tailored (4,2,7)
8 Freedom (7)
9 Puzzle involving pictures and letters (5)
10 Increased (4)
11 Act of mercy (8)
13 Add fuel (to) (5)
14 Villain – card (5)
19 Walking (8)
21 Eye infection (4)
23 Jacket (5)
24 Miles away (from) (1,3,3)
25 Vanishing act (13)

Down

1 Spanish Mediterranean port (6)
2 The authority on the British nobility (7)
3 Mountain lake (4)
4 Insect with transparent wings (6)
5 Bitterness (8)
6 Of the town (5)
7 Tries – writings (6)
12 Small round headgear (8)
15 Papal state (7)
16 Woven together (6)
17 Become involved (6)
18 Key in the text again (6)
20 Unexpected extra (5)
22 Katherine, wife number six (4)

88

Across

1 Obliging to the locals (11)
9 Young hare (7)
10 Tree (5)
11 Silhouette of buildings and land (7)
12 Woody valley (4)
13 Little Ronald (3)
15 Greek philosopher (5)
17 Northeast African country (5)
18 A corner stone of the British welfare state (3)
20 Vein of metal ore (4)
21 Belgian university town (7)
25 Stratum (5)
26 Person pursuing the alternative lifestyle (7)
27 Flag of the Royal Navy (5,6)

Down

2 Messenger (5)
3 Force defending a town (8)
4 Edible fat (6)
5 Unattractive (4)
6 Stealing (7)
7 Money given to or for the poor (4)
8 Swiss hut (6)
14 Vague (8)
15 How Keats's Knight at arms loitered (6)
16 London thoroughfare and theatre (7)
19 Thick mixture of liquid and solids (6)
22 In the middle of (5)
23 Short letter (4)
24 Legal summons (4)

Across

1 Daze (6)
4 Calm (6)
9 Polish dance (7)
10 European capital (5)
11 Girl's name (5)
12 Fish (that can be tightly packed!) (7)
13 Early stage (11)
18 Relating to the fingers (7)
20 Small wood (5)
22 Step (5)
23 Live longer than (7)
24 Form of Roman Catholic devotion (6)
25 Plant of the parsley family eaten as a vegetable (6)

Down

1 Fall down (6)
2 WWI Australian or New Zealand soldier (5)
3 Cut short (7)
5 Person with a disease of the skin (5)
6 Person or animal with a message? (7)
7 Walt, the animator (6)
8 Soft sweet (11)
14 Fall back (7)
15 Article of clothing (7)
16 Senior journalist (6)
17 Relating to the teeth (6)
19 Royal house (5)
21 Not complicated (5)

90

Across

1 Timid (5-7)
9 Happen again (5)
10 Lands in the sea (7)
11 Part of the leg (4)
12 (Nautically) get up! (4,1,3)
14 Deliberate and unprovoked (6)
15 (Of time) pass (6)
18 Share of profit (8)
20 Neat and tidy (4)
22 One who's bothered about problems (7)
23 Edible bulb (5)
24 Cough mixture (7,5)

Down

2 Sale (7)
3 Roman emperor (4)
4 Distance above the ground (6)
5 "___ That Ends Well" (4,4)
6 Relating to music, colour, or language (5)
7 Falling-out (12)
8 One whose wife is away (5,7)
13 One's often looked at in a bowl! (8)
16 Outskirts (7)
17 Remove outer covering (6)
19 Cause of disease (5)
21 Conservative (4)

Across

1 Marked (13)
8 Consume (3)
9 Pieces of supporting publicity (5)
10 Piece of supporting underwear (3)
11 Wanderer (5)
13 Candour (7)
15 Of a lifestyle centred on riding (6)
16 Office (6)
19 Piece of kitchen furniture (7)
21 Part of a coat (5)
22 Immature animal (3)
24 Piece of golf course turf (5)
25 Indian state (3)
26 After this one there are two to go to the club house (9,4)

Down

1 Prepare for action (5,3,5)
2 Little Arthur (3)
3 Attack the reputation (of) – see rasp (anag) (7)
4 Instructed (6)
5 It's exuded by some trees (5)
6 Cry (3)
7 Suit yourself! (2,2,3,6)
12 Border (5)
14 Use a broom (5)
17 Open (a door) (7)
18 Established as a fact (6)
20 Move obsequiously (5)
23 Container (3)
25 Sticky gunge (3)

92

Across

6 Bauble (7)
7 War against unbelievers (5)
8 How they lived ever after? (7)
9 With a tendency towards (3,2)
11 The Bible (9)
14 Self-control (9)
17 The baby bird! (5)
18 Light rain (7)
19 Conspicuous success (5)
20 Not the rough (7)

Down

1 Wide (as water in Norfolk?) (5)
2 Marsh bird (5)
3 Warlike (9)
4 Proverbially clinging creatures (7)
5 Assault (by the Royal Artillery?) (7)
10 One who keeps the books (9)
12 Classical gateway (7)
13 Part of highland dress (7)
15 Bright blue (5)
16 Launch on the Stock Exchange (5)

Across

1 Complete disorder (5)
4 Sunshade (7)
8 Drink (3)
9 Girl's name (5)
10 Short drama (7)
11 Absolutely not drunk as a lord! (5,2,1,5)
14 Still (3)
16 Odds (5)
17 River that joins the Severn at Chepstow (3)
19 A long, long way! (5,3,5)
21 Not active (7)
23 Recess (5)
24 Dismissed (3)
25 The Devil (7)
26 The Devil (5)

Down

1 Fairground target (7)
2 Tumbler (7)
3 White-collar employees (8,5)
4 Vigour (3)
5 Later changes (13)
6 Firm (5)
7 Milky coffee (5)
12 Lustre (5)
13 Chap (involved in the Gunpowder Plot?) (3)
15 Old Testament priest (3)
17 Small ferocious feline – prospect for oil (7)
18 Oriental (7)
19 Award (5)
20 Words to a song (5)
22 Hill – rocky peak (3)

94

Across

1 Diplomatic message — reminder (4-7)
9 Clumsy (3-6)
10 Play on words (3)
11 Paved area by a house (5)
13 Lever worked by foot (7)
14 Prime number (6)
15 Preserve (a body) from decay (6)
18 Drainage ways (7)
20 Proverbially, like a whistle! (5)
21 Bring an action against (3)
22 Without distinction between male and female (9)
24 Educational institution (5,6)

Down

2 Particular ideology (3)
3 Event (7)
4 Property of a dead person (6)
5 One who is getting on (5)
6 Disown (9)
7 Pastoral worker (11)
8 Mix (11)
12 Diagnosis should lead to it (9)
16 The Scottish play (7)
17 Notices (6)
19 Place regularly visited (5)
23 Flying saucer? (1,1,1)

Across

5 Loose dress (5)
8 Active person (4,4)
9 Express contempt (at) (5)
10 Put off (8)
11 Bubbles (5)
14 Mad cow disease (1,1,1)
16 Water heater (6)
17 Uniform for domestic servants (6)
18 (Of humour) subtle and matter-of-fact (3)
20 Soft fruit (5)
24 Forgiven (8)
25 Proverbially strong alloy (5)
26 Make-believe (8)
27 Facade (5)

Down

1 Waste food (5)
2 Stop (whatever it is you're doing), my hearties! (5)
3 Steal (with a credit card?) (5)
4 Tendencies (6)
6 Tree or shrub found in tropical swamps (8)
7 Animate being (8)
12 Academic term (8)
13 Fish (8)
14 Place of rest (3)
15 English cathedral city (3)
19 Burns or the Bruce? (6)
21 Biter (5)
22 Like a sheep (5)
23 Inactive person (5)

96

Across

1 Footwear (4)
3 Disinfectant (8)
8 Annoy (4)
9 Person who defends a position (8)
11 Thin and weak (5-5)
14 Searched for (6)
15 Girl's name (6)
17 Inclination to attack (10)
20 Pronouce the letter H (8)
21 Rounded lump (4)
22 New York state prison (4,4)
23 Cry loudly (4)

Down

1 (Of a woman) aggressively assertive (8)
2 Person of enormous importance (8)
4 Attraction (6)
5 One concerned with processes within living organisms (10)
6 Swimming pool (4)
7 Complain (about the fish?) (4)
10 Old Greek mathematician (10)
12 Badges (8)
13 Anthropophagite (8)
16 Sea god (6)
18 Girl (4)
19 (Part of) bridge (4)

Across

6 Confidence from the bottle? (5,7)

8 Modern (6)

9 Drinking vessel (6)

10 Dignified (7)

11 Part of a leg (5)

13 Part of a gun (5)

15 Small chocolate cake with nuts (7)

17 Currency unit (6)

19 Illusion (6)

20 I have no idea! (3,2,7)

Down

1 Accidental (12)

2 Motionless (2,4)

3 Inventor of the jet engine (7)

4 Grave (4)

5 Breakdown in a relationship (6)

7 Good things for gardeners! (5,7)

12 Red (7)

14 Line of figures (6)

16 Deserving (6)

18 Five hundred sheets of paper (4)

98

Across

1 England's largest lake (10)
7 Upset (7)
8 Multiplied by (5)
10 Thin fog (4)
11 With most of the sky clouded (8)
13 European country (6)
15 Soft colour (6)
17 Many (8)
18 Dirty foam (4)
21 Girl's name (5)
22 Luxurious railway carriage (7)
23 Measure for precious metals (4,6)

Down

1 Passes through the air (5)
2 African river (4)
3 Vegetable (6)
4 Motherly (8)
5 Piece left over (7)
6 Outstanding position (10)
9 Colony (10)
12 Written guarantee (8)
14 Person on a walk (7)
16 Flexible (6)
19 Heavenly body (5)
20 Hard work (4)

Across

1 Very small amount of money (8)
5 Hitler's party (4)
9 Father of Jacob and Esau (5)
10 Wear (7)
11 Second sight (12)
13 Three times (6)
14 At one (6)
17 Definitely not a rich uncle! (4,8)
20 Irritated (7)
21 German philosopher, 1770-1831 (5)
22 Suggestion (4)
23 Nerve pain (8)

Down

1 Stuck-up person (4)
2 It comes after a car but before a film! (7)
3 Area where on some days the sun never rises (or sets) (6,6)
4 Split – stick (6)
6 From the Far East (5)
7 Malicious 22 (8)
8 Burke or Hare, for example (12)
12 Just about (2,1,5)
15 Idea (7)
16 Develop wing feathers (6)
18 Cinema (5)
19 Misfortunes (4)

100

Across

1 Scruff of the neck (4)
3 Branch (8)
9 Prisoner (7)
10 Notions (5)
11 Borough and port in Co. Antrim (5)
12 Regularly alter direction (6)
14 Plant with highly coloured flowers (13)
17 Make a mistake (4,2)
19 Scottish peak of over 3,000 ft (5)
22 Informal language (5)
23 Concentrated (7)
24 Life after death? (8)
25 Close (4)

Down

1 Ornamental chain (8)
2 Musician (5)
4 0° C (8,5)
5 Arm support (5)
6 With the hand above the shoulder (7)
7 Job (4)
8 Several – people who take the plunge! (6)
13 Shameless (8)
15 Set free (7)
16 One descended from a son of Noah – I'm Thea (anag) (6)
18 Heathen (5)
20 Beethoven's last complete symphony (5)
21 Land in water (4)

Across

6 Country lover? (7)
7 Rented holiday home abroad? (5)
8 Customer (6)
9 Comfort (6)
10 Approximately 15 millilitre measurement in cooking (10)
12 Out-of-date (10)
16 Riches (6)
17 Rectangular (6)
18 Peculiar (5)
19 In the dock? (7)

Down

1 Brief journey – witty remark (5)
2 Ordained minister (6)
3 It's used for oral hygiene (10)
4 Bit of encouragement (6)
5 Voter (7)
9 Person no longer having any influence (5,5)
11 Innocent young woman (7)
13 Just ticking over (6)
14 State of great sorrow (6)
15 Heavenly messenger (5)

102

Across

1 Sheriff's assistant (6)
4 Frightened (6)
8 Digital growths (5)
9 Region of the Czech Republic, capital Brno (7)
10 Rash fellow (7)
11 Himalayan republic (5)
12 Wherewithal (9)
17 Austrian composer, 1732-1809 (5)
19 Boy's name (7)
21 Sleep (7)
22 Widespread dislike (5)
23 Look at (6)
24 Arrival of large numbers (6)

Down

1 Small boat ... (6)
2 ... and the rope for securing it (7)
3 Liking (for) (5)
5 (Of a medical condition) not acute (7)
6 Press the accelerator (3,2)
7 Lethal (6)
9 Season of madness? (9)
13 Bank across a river mouth (7)
14 Breed of dog (7)
15 Strong drink taken with beer (6)
16 Intense culmination (6)
18 Youthful (5)
20 Hit on the head (5)

Across

5 Street in Central Glasgow (11)
7 Old Liberal (4)
8 Zephyr, classically (4,4)
9 The end (7)
11 Worthless rubbish (5)
13 Deceit (5)
14 Communication (7)
16 There used to be 20 to the £ (8)
17 English spa city (4)
18 Kind of milk (11)

Down

1 Breathing organ (4)
2 (Of the weather) unsettled (7)
3 Stop (5)
4 Madame Tussaud's, for example (8)
5 Academic achievement (11)
6 Far-seeing? (4-7)
10 Impersonal (8)
12 Mendicants (7)
15 Underground worker (5)
17 Small tree (4)

104

Across

5 Dirty business! (9)
8 Berkshire college (4)
9 Adversary (8)
10 Deplorably bad (6)
11 Kind of sweet (6)
13 Dagger sign (6)
15 Pudding (6)
16 Snowstorm (8)
18 Stick (of sugar?) (4)
19 First version (9)

Down

1 Appreciative (and relieved?) (8)
2 Parchment roll (6)
3 Small writing fluid container (6)
4 Small bird – big architect (4)
6 Volcanic island north of Sicily (9)
7 Person of lower status (9)
12 Something rewritten from a rough version (4,4)
14 Bats (6)
15 Until now (2,4)
17 0 (4)

Across

 1 Full of pity (13)
 8 E.M., the writer (7)
 9 Reactionary and pompous person (5)
10 Correct text (4)
11 American comedian, 1880-1946 (1,1,6)
13 Flower (5)
14 Concur (5)
19 A virtue (of Gilbert and Sullivan?) (8)
21 Store – betray (4)
23 Bend (5)
24 Student (7)
25 Awkwardness (13)

Down

 1 Hot drink (6)
 2 Warlike (7)
 3 Aesthetic? (4)
 4 Neat and tidy (6)
 5 Pre-Redbrick? (8)
 6 Shakespearean fairy (5)
 7 City on the Rio Grande (2,4)
12 Ancestor (8)
15 Enrich (7)
16 Native American (6)
17 Charybdis's monstrous partner (6)
18 Enthusiasm (6)
20 Pulsate (5)
22 Legislation (4)

106

Across

1 Refrigeration facility (4,7)
9 Try (7)
10 Fur (5)
11 Needle (7)
12 Prospect (4)
13 Fix dishonestly (3)
15 Cured pig meat (5)
17 Recover one's strength (5)
18 Knock lightly (3)
20 Temperature (4)
21 Roman C (7)
25 Not clear (5)
26 Breastbone (7)
27 Part of a theatre (5,6)

Down

2 Exterior (5)
3 Prevailing (8)
4 Reel (6)
5 Danger (4)
6 Important archangel (7)
7 Fish – voice (4)
8 It's usually a struggle to make this up! (6)
14 Impressiveness of style (8)
15 Act properly (6)
16 Old cavalry horse (7)
19 Medicinal drugs (archaic) (6)
22 Kidney-related (5)
23 Rounded roof (4)
24 Dregs (4)

Across

1 Without compassion (13)
8 Make something last longer (3)
9 Famous (5)
10 Did 14! (3)
11 Having six equal square sides (5)
13 Siblings (7)
15 Attacker (6)
16 Muslim civil and religious leader (6)
19 Given a job (7)
21 Go for a swim (5)
22 Inferior (3)
24 A sheep's complaint? (5)
25 A long way (3)
26 Pre-1832 Reform Act constituency (6,7)

Down

1 Trader in second-hand vehicles (4-3,6)
2 Bishopric (3)
3 Eyeglass (7)
4 Painter (6)
5 Hell (5)
6 Tug (3)
7 Is very expensive (5,3,5)
12 Carry here (5)
14 Have objective reality (5)
17 Judge (7)
18 Part of speech (6)
20 Wall at one end of a ridged roof (5)
23 Intelligence (3)
25 Viral infection (3)

108

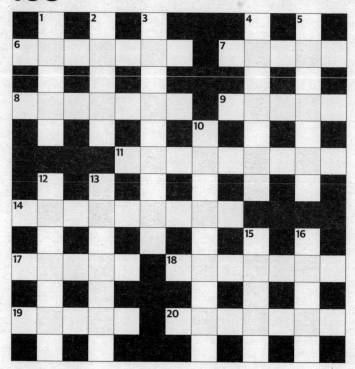

Across

6 Stare at closely (7)
7 Follow (5)
8 WWII POW camp near Leipzig (7)
9 Slow moving tropical mammal that hangs from trees (5)
11 Heavy attack (9)
14 Timetable of events (9)
17 Look pleased (5)
18 More hirsute (7)
19 Vessel for liquid (5)
20 Building (7)

Down

1 Poet who was "mad, bad and dangerous to know" (5)
2 Tolerate – stay (5)
3 Irishman from the northeast (9)
4 European language (7)
5 Protective care (7)
10 Areas around agricultural buildings (9)
12 Collapse (7)
13 Eternally youthful (7)
15 Small rented farm (5)
16 Fish (5)

Across

1 Accept willingly (as a cat?) (3,2)
4 Greenery (7)
8 Before the present (3)
9 Building or decorating craftsman (5)
10 In weeds (anag) (7)
11 Turning around (and upside down!) (13)
14 ... and not ... (3)
16 Eject (5)
17 Cereal plant (3)
19 Pasternak novel (6,7)
21 Pronounced (7)
23 Marriage (5)
24 What we breathe (3)
25 Benin, formerly (7)
26 Rub out (5)

Down

1 Subsequently (5,2)
2 Unnecessary fuss (7)
3 Geometrical figure (13)
4 Enemy (3)
5 Woman who lunches? (4,2,7)
6 The soul (5)
7 Abrasive powder (5)
12 Precious stone (5)
13 Flooded valley – Spanish estuary (3)
15 Expression of surprise (3)
17 Wind instrument (7)
18 Defeat thoroughly (7)
19 Celtic priest (5)
20 Trap (5)
22 24 hours (3)

Across

1 Suet pudding (7,4)
9 Chronicler (9)
10 President Lincoln (3)
11 Polynesian island state (5)
13 Singer like Bing (7)
14 Person who plays old stringed instrument (6)
15 Smear with goo (6)
18 Lookout (7)
20 Relating to the extreme north or south (5)
21 11th-century Bishop of Bayeux (3)
22 Made up of several elements (9)
24 Roman emperor (11)

Down

2 Liquid produced in infected tissue (3)
3 Inhabitants of ancient city of Asia Minor (7)
4 Show clearly (6)
5 Australian wild dog (5)
6 Old body armour (5,4)
7 Brief halt on an election tour (7-4)
8 Small round grains of ground cereal (5,6)
12 13th-century Italian traveller to China (5,4)
16 Make use of (7)
17 Southern part of Ukraine (6)
19 Folds (5)
23 Electrically charged molecule (3)

Across

5 Common English family name (5)
8 Abrasive pad (4,4)
9 Part of a wicket (5)
10 Disregarding of one's own interests (8)
11 Greek letter (5)
14 Everything (3)
16 Mature – happy (6)
17 Season of the year (6)
18 It gets laid (3)
20 Wind instrument (5)
24 Belonging to the underworld (8)
25 Someone with an alternative lifestyle (5)
26 Precious metal, Pt (8)
27 Little Penelope (5)

Down

1 Screw up (5)
2 Yours is me! (5)
3 Ridged fabric (5)
4 Animal remains preserved in stone (6)
6 Severely damage (8)
7 Small fairy-tale hero (3,5)
12 24 conflagration (8)
13 State of panic (4,4)
14 Reverence (3)
15 Fall behind (3)
19 Soft – kind (6)
21 Pier (5)
22 Upturned (2,3)
23 Ascend (5)

Across

1 "Wuthering Heights" hero (10)
7 Playtime? (7)
8 An argument has at least two! (5)
10 Advance payment (4)
11 Resort on the Costa del Sol (8)
13 Ligaments (6)
15 Flushed in complexion (6)
17 Hamlet's home (8)
18 Study for an exam (4)
21 Give up (5)
22 Relating to the abdomen (7)
23 Aircraft's course (6,4)

Down

1 Spartan serf (5)
2 Assistant (4)
3 Period of greatest success (6)
4 Result of a stroke of bad luck? (4,4)
5 Violinist – fraudster (7)
6 Bundle of cut cereal (found at the pub?) (5,5)
9 Complete stoppage (10)
12 Final performance (8)
14 Breathing hole (7)
16 Shrub used for hedges (6)
19 Value (5)
20 Ancient South American (4)

Across

1 Soundness (8)
5 Devotional painting of a holy figure (4)
9 Negative quantity (5)
10 Proverbially wise king (7)
11 Affection feigned for a purpose (8,4)
13 Scrape (6)
14 Ability quite out of the ordinary (6)
17 From birth (12)
20 Total flop (7)
21 Fruit (5)
22 Spanish painter, 1746-1828 (4)
23 Bossy woman (8)

Down

1 Seductive woman (4)
2 Listlessness (7)
3 Refusal to obey (12)
4 17th-century Dutch explorer of the Pacific (6)
6 Piece of oval jewellery with carved portrait (5)
7 Rubbish! (8)
8 As a nutcracker it is excessive! (12)
12 Canine guard (8)
15 Inadequately dressed (3-4)
16 Picture house (6)
18 Upper-class – smart – all male Clarks? (5)
19 Soon (4)

114

Across

1 Influence (4)
3 Man from Glasgow, perhaps (8)
9 White crystalline substance used in cold medicines (7)
10 Less frequently seen (5)
11 Actor, Henry or Jane (5)
12 Totting up (6)
14 Person or thing used to mask the real purpose (8,5)
17 Frozen plain (6)
19 Animals (that must be separated from sheep) (5)
22 Chemical – inert (anag) (5)
23 Rescue (7)
24 Pustular scar (8)
25 Despatch (4)

Down

1 CO, perhaps (8)
2 Fruit (is the answer!) (5)
4 Warm-up for the main event (7-6)
5 Weary (5)
6 Seafarer (7)
7 Scene of a naval mutiny, 1797 (4)
8 Got smaller (6)
13 Framework for sleep (8)
15 Watery (7)
16 Bargain (6)
18 Vision (5)
20 Alert (5)
21 Break – card game (4)

Across

6 Ready mixed alcoholic drink for the young (7)
7 Musical work (5)
8 Bill of prices (6)
9 Object of superstition (6)
10 Cemetery (10)
12 Voyeur (7,3)
16 Origin (6)
17 Cattle food (6)
18 Religious song (5)
19 Eye specialist (7)

Down

1 Dwell on one's own triumphs (5)
2 Representation of an astrological system (6)
3 Where rivers meet (10)
4 With acne (6)
5 Rubbing out (7)
9 In confrontation (4,2,4)
11 Great courage (7)
13 Stout (6)
14 Centre (6)
15 Dog's lead (5)

116

Across

1 Hive of activity (6)
4 European country (6)
8 From A to Z? (5)
9 Showing envious resentment (7)
10 English economist with views on population, 1766-1834 (7)
11 Acquisitiveness (5)
12 Get back again (9)
17 Jottings (5)
19 Sudden urge (7)
21 Fish (7)
22 Consider (5)
23 Interfere (with) (6)
24 – (6)

Down

1 Having too many wives (6)
2 Piece of embroidery (7)
3 Door fastening (5)
5 Argument (7)
6 (Make a) low humming sound (5)
7 End of a rugby game (2,4)
9 Piece of incense (4,5)
13 Handguns (7)
14 Egotistical (7)
15 Rousing song (6)
16 Undermine (6)
18 Subject to the rise and fall of the sea (5)
20 Paste used to hold window glass (5)

Across

5 Snow slide (9)
8 Seaside structure (4)
9 Old toll road (8)
10 Agreement (6)
11 Proper (6)
13 Muslim women's garments (6)
15 Hard stone (6)
16 Turkish city on the Bosphorus (8)
18 Member of a religious community (4)
19 One seeking a job, say (9)

Down

1 Do too much (8)
2 Decorated with grooves (6)
3 Binder (anag) (6)
4 Fellow (4)
6 Written or spoken debate (9)
7 Miser (9)
12 Formal event with ritual (8)
14 With finesse (6)
15 Desire to harm (6)
17 European mountains (4)

118

Across

1 Emergency ending to a flight (6,7)
8 Brave (7)
9 Run swerving from left to right (5)
10 Ceremony (4)
11 Kind of primrose – kind of view (5-3)
13 Extremely happy situation (5)
14 Japan's imperial capital until 1868 (5)
19 Russian pianist, Vladimir, 1904-89 (8)
21 Small unit of length (4)
23 Tsarist decree (5)
24 Hot pepper sauce (7)
25 Government minister (4,9)

Down

1 Important person (6)
2 Akin (7)
3 Jacob's twin brother (4)
4 Baltic country, capital Riga (6)
5 Currently (8)
6 Angry (5)
7 Diving birds with long necks (6)
12 Without a blemish (8)
15 North African country (7)
16 In spite of (6)
17 Motionless (6)
18 Not easily pleased (6)
20 Domain (5)
22 Talented (4)

Across

1 Beauty of figure (11)
9 Bypass (7)
10 Long-legged bird (5)
11 Argue (7)
12 See – place (4)
13 Short-winged diving bird (3)
15 Welsh Wales (5)
17 Simpleton (5)
18 It often comes before "order" (3)
20 Lodgings (4)
21 Take back (7)
25 Glowing body of ignited gas (5)
26 Detach (7)
27 Read a clock (4,3,4)

Down

2 Red dye (5)
3 Mighty (8)
4 St Ignatius ____, founder of the Jesuits (6)
5 French Mediterranean resort (4)
6 Improve the effectiveness of a sword (or a pencil!) (7)
7 Middle Eastern country (4)
8 Part of a church (6)
14 KO (8)
15 Collect together systematically (6)
16 Change country or place of residence (7)
19 Ghost (6)
22 Scare (5)
23 Submissive (4)
24 Make better (4)

120

Across

1 Velasquez's Venus (6)
4 Oral (6)
9 Green vegetable (7)
10 Root vegetable (5)
11 Tell on (5)
12 Engage in an extreme winter sport – as I park (anag) (7)
13 Where you bring your own drink (6,5)
18 Cheat financially (7)
20 "___ of Athens" (5)
22 Money (to be found by muck) (5)
23 Joseph Conrad novel (4,3)
24 Conclusion (6)
25 Seabird that seems to "walk on water" (6)

Down

1 Withstand (6)
2 Sharp instrument (5)
3 (or [or { (7)
5 Difficult question (5)
6 Israeli parliament (7)
7 You can't get out this way! (2,4)
8 18th-century furniture-maker (11)
14 Curt in manner (7)
15 Phoenician goddess – stare at (anag) (7)
16 Fit for eating (6)
17 Paint with a smooth hard finish (6)
19 Fireraising (5)
21 Prime minister, 1990-97 (5)

Across

1 Those expelled from Heaven (6,6)
9 Vicars of Christ (5)
10 In the open air (7)
11 Protest strongly (against) (4)
12 Publisher's imprint (8)
14 Hired assassins (3,3)
15 Total chaos (6)
18 Small bunches of scented flowers (8)
20 " ___ and bear it" (4)
22 Not precise (7)
23 At exactly the right moment (2,3)
24 Status of having no experience of life at all (7,5)

Down

2 Put into a job (7)
3 Endure (4)
4 One of the group of political advisers to George W. Bush? (6)
5 Citizen of a particular country (8)
6 Historical period (5)
7 Resolute and determined (6-6)
8 Anxious and fearful (12)
13 Capital of Serbia (8)
16 French bean (7)
17 Evergreen shrub (6)
19 Perspiration (5)
21 Type of seagoing ferry (2-2)

122

Across

1 Cut of meat from the breast (7,2,4)
8 Centre of our universe (3)
9 Be of use (5)
10 Sheep (3)
11 Remove a restriction (5)
13 Of a system where many link together as one (7)
15 Struggle (6)
16 Main employment (3,3)
19 One bringing a charge (7)
21 Drunk (5)
22 Steal (3)
24 "___ Andronicus" (5)
25 Expression of contempt (3)
26 Oliver Cromwell's title (4,9)

Down

1 Container for crackers? (7,6)
2 Public house (3)
3 Small falcon (7)
4 Economy (6)
5 Early psychoanalyst (5)
6 Part of the head (3)
7 He would sell 1 across (6,7)
12 Fundamental (5)
14 Organise (something) differently (5)
17 Professional entertainer (7)
18 Small cave (6)
20 "___ and take notice" (3,2)
23 Watering hole (3)
25 Small amount (3)

123

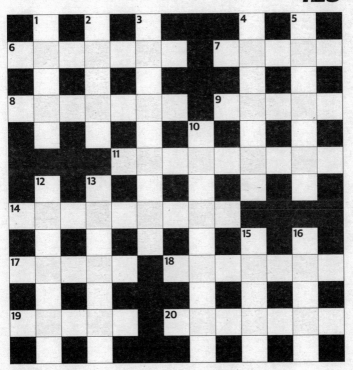

Across

6 Ancient Egyptian king (7)
7 Make swollen (with food?) (5)
8 Condition (7)
9 Stock market disaster (5)
11 It's a hit! (9)
14 Kind of male grouse (9)
17 Small illustration as part of another (5)
18 It's often by the door (7)
19 Fad (5)
20 Green stone (7)

Down

1 County (5)
2 Native American warrior (5)
3 Children's game involving marked squares (9)
4 Flower seller (7)
5 Wind instrument (7)
10 Geographical proper noun (5,4)
12 (Of a session) attended by all participants (7)
13 Musical movement (7)
15 Fright(en) (5)
16 Answer (5)

124

Across

1 Animal skins (5)
4 Talks volubly (7)
8 Definite article (3)
9 South American beaver-like animal (5)
10 Bring up carefully (7)
11 Never-ending problems (3,2,8)
14 Marry (3)
16 Sinks below the surface (5)
17 Constituent of varnish, sealing wax etc (3)
19 Class of boxer (13)
21 Characteristic of a class (7)
23 Stroll (5)
24 Contribute (something) (3)
25 Betrayal of country (7)
26 Foe (5)

Down

1 Fine-toothed blade (7)
2 Terra firma (3,4)
3 Pompous asses (7,6)
4 Desire (3)
5 Cruel and debauched French nobleman (7,2,4)
6 With the same value (5)
7 Appears (5)
12 Stream (5)
13 When one expects to be there (1,1,1)
15 Look at (3)
17 Clear to the reader (7)
18 Knives and forks etc (7)
19 Struggle (5)
20 Girl with a gun? (5)
22 Tin (3)

Across

1 Unfriendly (5-6)
9 £ (5,4)
10 Hairstyle (3)
11 Seaside golf course (5)
13 Clear (7)
14 Lady's formal greeting with a 10 (6)
15 Bleach (6)
18 He is after animal fur (7)
20 Samuel Beckett's awaited character (5)
21 Witchcraft (3)
22 Deep round hollow in the hills (9)
24 As happy as can be! (4,7)

Down

2 Greek letter T (3)
3 They wear no clothes for pleasure (7)
4 Lionel Bart musical (6)
5 Moulds, mushrooms etc (5)
6 Dominated (9)
7 Sustained effort (to find a job?) (11)
8 With stubbornness (11)
12 Story (9)
16 Topper (for a snob?) (4,3)
17 English-speaking foreigner in Latin America (6)
19 He's supposed to be learning (5)
23 Possess (3)

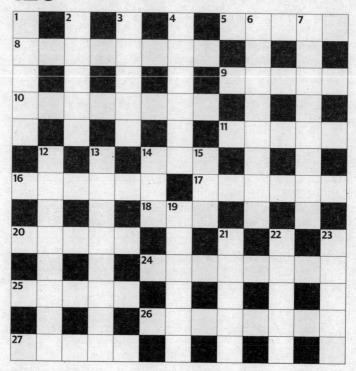

Across

5 Ostentatious (5)
8 Close partner (8)
9 Pig-speak (5)
10 Asian country, capital Islamabad (8)
11 Areas of substandard housing (5)
14 The key to life! (1,1,1)
16 Attack (6)
17 Very last scene (6)
18 Other than – only (3)
20 Colour (5)
24 Fraudulent person (8)
25 Corrupt (5)
26 Mythical sailor (8)
27 Reptile (in the grass?) (5)

Down

1 Deep fried potatoes (5)
2 Quench (5)
3 Members of a Mennonite sect in the US (5)
4 Reach (6)
6 One employed casually for menial tasks (8)
7 It harnesses natural energy (8)
12 Prime number (8)
13 Snag (8)
14 Inexperienced young woman in fashionable society (3)
15 Stern of a ship (3)
19 Into the sky (6)
21 Irritate (5)
22 Cold and unfriendly (5)
23 Make one's living as an author (5)

Across

1 Source of heat (4)
3 Contemptuous (8)
8 Single item (4)
9 Hit repeatedly with a heavy stick (8)
11 With leaves removed (10)
14 Prosper (6)
15 Spanish fleet (6)
17 In a birthday suit? (5,5)
20 Removal (which is good!) (8)
21 Welsh darling – German composer (4)
22 Give out (8)
23 Cut (4)

Down

1 Ease of change (8)
2 Cost of ticket (4,4)
4 Vault (6)
5 False trail (3,7)
6 Know inwardly (4)
7 Small road (4)
10 Commerce made illegal by the UK in 1807 (5,5)
12 Negative reaction (8)
13 Privation (8)
16 Small spring flower, growing from a corm (6)
18 Engendered (4)
19 Chances (4)

128

Across

6 Welcome beacon to a returning mariner (7,5)
8 Wait (on) (6)
9 Slender and fragile — 1960s' supermodel (6)
10 From Valparaiso, perhaps (7)
11 Oil-bearing rock (5)
13 Italian island resort (5)
15 Direction finder (7)
17 Small church (6)
19 Bribe (6)
20 Explanation of something (new) to an audience (12)

Down

1 Kind of moorland plant (5,7)
2 Eric Blair (6)
3 It shows the way (to peace in the Middle East?) (4,3)
4 Mild expletive (4)
5 End (6)
7 Easily upset (6,6)
12 Old institution for young offenders (7)
14 Rest (6)
16 Open to all (6)
18 Connect(ion) (4)

Across

1 Harry Houdini's trade (10)
7 Keep going! (7)
8 Stories (5)
10 Sharp taste (4)
11 Alternative to a knocker (8)
13 Walking (2,4)
15 Worn at the edges (6)
17 Harriet Beecher Stowe's black hero (5,3)
18 God of thunder (4)
21 Dismay (5)
22 Remote (7)
23 Absolute bounder! (10)

Down

1 King of Northumbria, 616-33 (5)
2 Farm vehicle (4)
3 Moving part in an internal combustion engine (6)
4 To do with books (8)
5 Institution displaying pictures (7)
6 Coming from the north (10)
9 Togetherness (10)
12 Relating to the home (8)
14 Objective (7)
16 Fast food item (3,3)
19 Squirrel away (5)
20 Very large land mass (4)

130

Across

1 One in a swimming school? (8)
5 Crustacean (caught while rowing?) (4)
9 Edgar Allan Poe's bird (5)
10 Written heading (7)
11 With the right balance (12)
13 Vacillate (on the brink?) (6)
14 Horror-struck (6)
17 Results of actions (12)
20 Figures indicating the movement of average values (7)
21 Have an obligation (to) (5)
22 Essential meaning (4)
23 Deliberate (8)

Down

1 Leave a car somewhere (4)
2 Go backwards (7)
3 Ubiquity (12)
4 Safe (6)
6 Act like a monarch (5)
7 Triteness (8)
8 Salad vegetables (6,6)
12 Leg covering (8)
15 Person taking an eye for an eye (7)
16 Chase (6)
18 Points in a diagram where lines intersect (5)
19 Horse breeding establishment (4)

Across

1 Throw (4)
3 Prudent (8)
9 Sale made to buy something more expensive and better (5-2)
10 Goddess of love (5)
11 Gentleman's gentleman (5)
12 Pen for livestock in North America (OK?) (6)
14 Holding to personal principles (4,2,7)
17 Girl's name (6)
19 Theatrical show (5)
22 Alcoholic drink (slang) (5)
23 Get by transmission from the past (7)
24 Relegate to a minor position (8)
25 Lump of earth (4)

Down

1 Smarten up (8)
2 Play for time (5)
4 Spitting (13)
5 Cut in two (5)
6 Medical dressing (7)
7 Compass point (4)
8 Disappear at once! (4,2)
13 Mannered (8)
15 Not being the object of any affection (7)
16 Unrefined in manner (6)
18 Linked to a monarch (5)
20 Of illness caused by molecules multiplying within one (5)
21 Long-billed wading bird (4)

132

Across

6 Refuge (7)
7 West Country river (5)
8 French wine (found in the churchyard?) (6)
9 Group aiming to dissuade strike-breakers (6)
10 Property (4,6)
12 Appease (10)
16 Person hunting birds (6)
17 One with special knowledge (6)
18 English poet, 1795-1821 (5)
19 Outrage (7)

Down

1 Nautical map (5)
2 Bright (6)
3 Secret swan (anag) (10)
4 Talisman (6)
5 Dignified grandeur (7)
9 Quality of being widespread (10)
11 Cavalryman (who swears a lot?) (7)
13 Civil (6)
14 Swell (6)
15 In Greek mythology, king of Troy (5)

Across

5 Carbonated drink (4,5)
8 God of war (4)
9 Exhausted (4,4)
10 Winding sheet (6)
11 (Of a reputation) show to be false (6)
13 Lozenge-shaped knitting pattern (6)
15 From Damascus? (6)
16 Twice the radius (8)
18 Near (4)
19 Parade of troops before a prominent figure (5,4)

Down

1 Role of the office junior? (8)
2 Covered with stuffing (6)
3 Chance (6)
4 Part of speech (4)
6 Purging of the emotions (9)
7 It measures precipitation (4,5)
12 Noblewoman (8)
14 Lead astray (6)
15 Angel (6)
17 If a sufficient one, it could be square! (4)

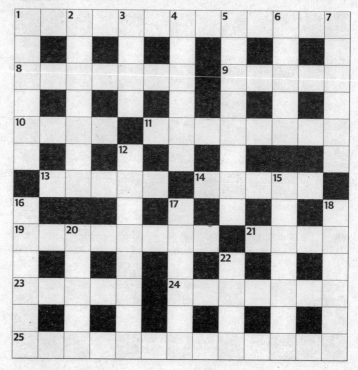

Across

1 Success that will not be repeated (5,2,3,3)

8 Short post for tying a rope to (7)

9 Legendary king of Crete (5)

10 Singing voice (4)

11 Relating to general office work (8)

13 Path of a celestial body (5)

14 Mirror (5)

19 Um and er (8)

21 Fluctuate (2-2)

23 Madness (5)

24 Letters received by a public figure (7)

25 In a very impressive way (13)

Down

1 Member of a left-of-centre society (6)

2 Composed entirely of out-standing performers (3-4)

3 Chief — part of the body (4)

4 Little rounded swelling (6)

5 Devolution of government to a region (4,4)

6 Relating to ancient Carthage (5)

7 Settle down comfortably (6)

12 Harass — divert (8)

15 Dribble (7)

16 Topics (6)

17 Kind of energy (6)

18 Disguised off break from a right-arm bowler (6)

20 Meaning (5)

22 Medicinal tablet (4)

Across

1 Not absolute (11)
9 Fine mesh – the rain (anag) (7)
10 Pretend (3,2)
11 Otalgia (7)
12 Encourage (4)
13 Confederate soldier in the American Civil War (3)
15 Female (5)
17 Ring next to the bull (5)
18 Unit of work (3)
20 Renown (4)
21 Going to the root of things (7)
25 He walks by himself (5)
26 Uncertain (7)
27 Minor disagreement (11)

Down

2 Willow used for making baskets (5)
3 Fruit of a conifer (4,4)
4 Somewhat (6)
5 Lofty (4)
6 Person of experience (7)
7 Footwear (4)
8 With the clutch engaged (2,4)
14 Easily influenced (8)
15 Empty talk (6)
16 Something kept as a reminder (7)
19 It's not a good thing to bear one! (6)
22 Childhood breathing difficulty (5)
23 Catalogue (4)
24 Worry (4)

136

Across

1 Engagement (6)
4 Hat worn in 1 across (6)
9 Furrier (7)
10 Having a hemispherical roof (5)
11 Fantastic (5)
12 Officer of a royal household (7)
13 Bureau (7,4)
18 Bird (7)
20 Snarling sound (5)
22 Spicy Cajun chicken or seafood soup (5)
23 Eat nuts (anag) (7)
24 Occupier (6)
25 Avid (6)

Down

1 Chess piece (6)
2 (Impart) pollution (5)
3 Not severe (7)
5 Kind of duck (5)
6 Where Martin Luther King was assassinated and Elvis is buried (7)
7 Slightly drunk (6)
8 Actions outside the law (11)
14 Prescribed combination of diet, exercise etc (7)
15 Sirius (3,4)
16 President Eisenhower's first name (6)
17 Covered by melting snow and ice (6)
19 From which a tall oak may grow (5)
21 Snow leopard (5)

Across

1 Person producing the lines for films etc (12)
9 Composition for nine players (5)
10 Deserving of sympathy (7)
11 Golf club (4)
12 I agree! (4,4)
14 Observe (6)
15 Insect (6)
18 Long journeys by sea (8)
20 Bounders (4)
22 Kind of window (7)
23 Deadly African snake (5)
24 Lethal grip? (12)

Down

2 Keep company (with) (7)
3 Very small amount (4)
4 Knocked lightly (6)
5 Slowed down (8)
6 Kind of steak (1-4)
7 Place that is booked (8,4)
8 US city hosting an annual 500-mile motor race (12)
13 Emperor Augustus's earlier name – vacation (anag) (8)
16 Confine (7)
17 Revoke – quash (6)
19 Indian stringed instrument (5)
21 Far Eastern nursemaid (4)

138

Across

1 Light summer meal (4,9)
8 Modern (3)
9 Small cat-like animal that smells! (5)
10 Animal skin with hair attached (3)
11 Artist's stand (5)
13 Slight wound (7)
15 Disquiet (6)
16 Severe trial (6)
19 To be expected (7)
21 (In law) right of ownership (5)
22 Acknowledgement of debt (1,1,1)
24 Boring tool (5)
25 Not yet dry (3)
26 European principality, capital Vaduz (13)

Down

1 Resultant (13)
2 Way to get out at cricket (1,1,1)
3 Shellfish (7)
4 Very generous (6)
5 Flower (5)
6 Washington-based world financial institution (1,1,1)
7 North Yorkshire town – where the English defeated the Scots in 1138 at the Battle of the Standard (13)
12 Bait for mackerel? (5)
14 River at Nottingham (5)
17 Comes back (7)
18 Pestilence (6)
20 Attain (5)
23 Small guitar (abbr) (3)
25 Grief (3)

Across

6 Enterprise (7)
7 Brief (5)
8 Rich fabric (7)
9 Fern leaf (5)
11 (Nautically) SS (9)
14 Beast of burden (9)
17 Strike (5)
18 Proverbially austere Greek (7)
19 Low joint (5)
20 Ravaged by fighting armies (3-4)

Down

1 Cheerful (5)
2 Unable to move (5)
3 Something that's handed down (9)
4 Treat with great care and affection (7)
5 Wild with worry (7)
10 Mammal that carries its young in a pouch (9)
12 Complete agreement (7)
13 Pin for bowling at (7)
15 Soup (5)
16 City on the Nile (5)

140

Across

1 Reserved and haughty (5)
4 Incursions (7)
8 Period of sexual activity for deer (3)
9 Female ruff (5)
10 Czech composer and nationalist, 1824-84 (7)
11 Not needing others (4-9)
14 London university college (1,1,1)
16 Powerful person (5)
17 Nourished (3)
19 Fertilising the fields organically (4-9)
21 Biting (7)
23 Moisten roasting meat with fat (5)
24 Historical period (3)
25 He took Jerusalem from the Christians in 1187 (7)
26 Sharp pulls (5)

Down

1 Insecticide dispenser (7)
2 Rest on top (of) (7)
3 Condiment (6,7)
4 Possessive pronoun (3)
5 Ruined Cistercian monastery in Yorkshire (8,5)
6 What Rhett Butler frankly couldn't give (1,4)
7 Tolerate (5)
12 West African country and river (5)
13 Before in time (poetic) (3)
15 Old French coin (3)
17 Shiver (7)
18 Bends (3-4)
19 Glandular disease (5)
20 Boy's name (5)
22 Light brown (3)

Across

1 Upper part of the stern of a warship (11)
9 Absolutely the same (9)
10 Mesh (3)
11 Severe (5)
13 Legendary Spanish lover (3,4)
14 Provoke to action (6)
15 Thin plate or layer (6)
18 Car's transmission mechanism (7)
20 In front (5)
21 Pull along with difficulty (3)
22 Clever (9)
24 Casual (11)

Down

2 Function (3)
3 Device preventing backward movement (7)
4 Old Spanish and Portuguese monetary unit (6)
5 American singer-songwriter, born 1941 (5)
6 Leading (to) (9)
7 Songbird (11)
8 Make uniform (11)
12 Oblong (9)
16 Anti (7)
17 O (6)
19 Give information and/or instructions to (5)
23 Belonging to us (3)

142

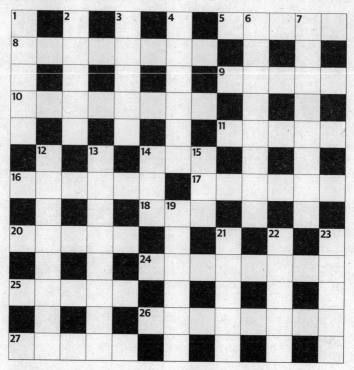

Across

5 Degrade (5)
8 Absolutely determined (4-4)
9 Goat – pot (5)
10 Left over (8)
11 Proposal to pay (5)
14 Church seat (3)
16 Fort (6)
17 Instead of (2,4)
18 Kitchen utensil (3)
20 Destroy (5)
24 Loud noise (8)
25 Secure a rope (5)
26 Hard Swiss cheese (8)
27 English county (5)

Down

1 Make a noise like a bird (5)
2 Remove explosively (5)
3 Dwelling (5)
4 Enter uninvited (6)
6 All but overflowing (8)
7 Plated like a mirror (8)
12 Bald (8)
13 Barrier of stakes (8)
14 Vim (3)
15 Succeed (3)
19 Self-possession (6)
21 Start (of something) (5)
22 Covered with coal dust (5)
23 With humour (5)

Across

1 It "springs eternal in the human breast" (4)
3 Sailing ship (8)
8 Harvest (4)
9 It's artificially curved for making chairs etc (8)
11 Celebration for victorious Oxford rowers (4,6)
14 Do something without restraint (3,3)
15 Old ship (6)
17 Occurring at random (3-3-4)
20 Flying an aircraft (8)
21 Opposed to (4)
22 Reprimands severely (8)
23 White meat (4)

Down

1 Wild flower (8)
2 Childhood companion (8)
4 Shudder-making (6)
5 Distinctly possible (2,3,5)
6 Sheltered spot (4)
7 Impolite (4)
10 Plant much favoured in Victorian halls (10)
12 Squirm (8)
13 Depending on the time of year (8)
16 Large (greedy) seabird (6)
18 Gemstone (4)
19 Edible mollusc (4)

144

Across

6 Someone from Merseyside (12)
8 Someone from Merseyside (6)
9 Tuber eaten as a vegetable (6)
10 Small crater in a road surface (7)
11 Digit (5)
13 Take illegally (5)
15 Submissive (7)
17 Mood (of anger?) (6)
19 From dawn to dusk (3,3)
20 Old voice conductor (8,4)

Down

1 Proverbially unintelligent gathering! (5,2,5)
2 Assert positively (6)
3 Well regulated (7)
4 Rubbish deposit (4)
5 Grasp (6)
7 Sure sign that winter is on the way (6,6)
12 Mixture (7)
14 Say again (6)
16 Parchment (6)
18 Incursion (4)

Across

1 Liquid measure (5,5)
7 Religious festival (4,3)
8 Consumed by fire (5)
10 Speed (4)
11 Where the neighbour lives? (4,4)
13 Barefooted (6)
15 Public platforms (6)
17 He does all the odd jobs (8)
18 Fish (4)
21 Sing in a voice alternating between normal and falsetto (5)
22 Further from the action (7)
23 Kind of beetle (that ticks!) (5-5)

Down

1 Undercut of beef (5)
2 Loosen (4)
3 Couch for resting on (3,3)
4 Relax and start speaking more freely (8)
5 Covered parking space (7)
6 With care and attention to detail (10)
9 Extremely worn (10)
12 Fluent in many languages (8)
14 (Of a meeting) adjourned indefinitely (Latin) (4,3)
16 Farm implement (6)
19 Mark with fine diagonal lines (5)
20 Leave out (4)

146

Across

1 Return to power, say (8)
5 In a frenzy (4)
9 Receiver of stolen goods (5)
10 With deep feelings (7)
11 Position of special prominence (5,2,5)
13 Skin preparation (6)
14 Deadly agent (6)
17 First day of Lent (3,9)
20 Ascribed (7)
21 Traveller (5)
22 Leading Regency architect (4)
23 Make economies (8)

Down

1 Part of a shirt (4)
2 Mosque tower (7)
3 Die by haemorrhaging (5,2,5)
4 Usage (6)
6 Cosa Nostra (5)
7 Irish county, home of two cats (8)
8 One or two? (5,2,5)
12 German shepherd (8)
15 Stop happening (with the foot?) (5,2)
16 Nervous (2,4)
18 Desires (5)
19 Commonly held belief that is untrue (4)

Across

1 Propel from behind (4)
3 Cold sweet (3,5)
9 Creature of myth (7)
10 Savoury jelly (5)
11 (Musically) with all performers (5)
12 Hearsay (6)
14 Flavoured preparation mixed with milk (7,6)
17 Unit for measuring the distances of stars (6)
19 Board game (5)
22 Lines from the centre of a circle (5)
23 Badly mannered (3-4)
24 All else depends on it (8)
25 Change direction (4)

Down

1 Couple it (anag) (8)
2 Garment (5)
4 Denial (13)
5 It can be staked! (5)
6 Explain in a certain way (7)
7 A lot (4)
8 Lady who rode naked through Coventry (6)
13 Someone fighting for a cause (8)
15 Someone to rely on in an emergency (7)
16 Beyond the range of understanding (6)
18 Sudden fine jet (5)
20 Eagle's nest (5)
21 Arduous journey (4)

148

Across

6 High scoring baseball hit (4,3)

7 Poison (5)

8 Personal ornament (6)

9 Caprice (6)

10 Parts of it are excellent (7,3)

12 Not at all central (10)

16 Accident (6)

17 As a 10 (6)

18 Predatory person or fish (5)

19 Piano! (7)

Down

1 South Africans of Dutch descent (5)

2 Of great fortitude (6)

3 Condition of being a writer (10)

4 One thing after another (6)

5 Transmit (something to) (7)

9 Tears two up (anag) (10)

11 Pleasure (7)

13 Remain firm (in something) (6)

14 Written communication (6)

15 Mammal that produces 9s (5)

Across

1 Hit hard (6)
4 Be plentiful (6)
8 Cat-speak (5)
9 Belief in central control of affairs (7)
10 Pygmalion's statue that was brought back to life – eat gal a (anag) (7)
11 Lock of hair (5)
12 Shakespeare's second of age of man (9)
17 Exam taken a second time (5)
19 The other way round (7)
21 African wild pig (7)
22 Small bloodsucking insects (5)
23 Kindly (6)
24 Gor ___ ! (6)

Down

1 Worship (6)
2 Infectious fever producing red spots (7)
3 Break out (5)
5 Lucky dip container (4,3)
6 Join together (5)
7 Death (6)
9 Adding herbs etc (9)
13 Hertfordshire town (7)
14 From which sailors were hanged (7)
15 Development (6)
16 Spirited (6)
18 Go away! (5)
20 Watching by night (5)

150

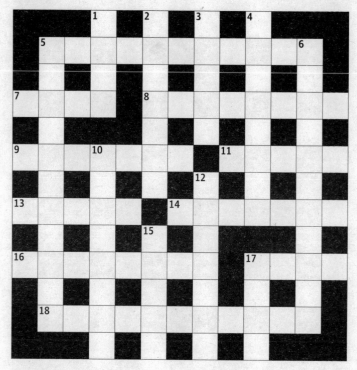

Across

5 Building showing the movements of the heavens (11)

7 Skewer used for roasting (4)

8 Deduce (8)

9 Educational establishment (7)

11 Stink (5)

13 Part of a flower (5)

14 Sully (7)

16 Not established as a fact (8)

17 Unhappy (4)

18 Garbage dump (7,4)

Down

1 Potty (4)

2 Greet with pleasure (7)

3 Hardly visible (5)

4 Infantry soldier (8)

5 Part of a serious smoker's kit (4,7)

6 Part of a wicket (6,5)

10 Invective (8)

12 Definitely stout (7)

15 Shun (5)

17 Complain (about the meat?) (4)

SOLUTIONS

1

2

3

4

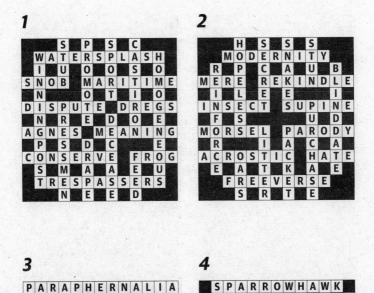

5

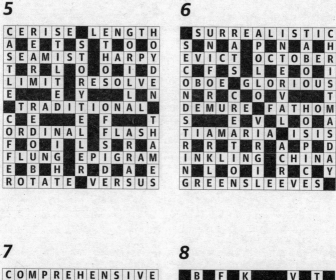

6

7

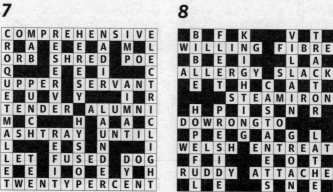

8

9

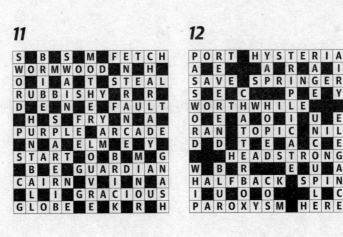

10

11

12

13

14

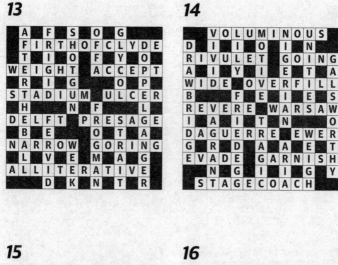

15

16

17

```
    C  A  H        S  P
 B  O  U  D  O  I  R     O  T  H  E  R
 U     V     G           A        N
 E  N  R  I  C  H     B  E  N  I  G  N
 T     S     S     Y     Z     U
       E  U  T  H  A  N  A  S  I  A     N
 B           R     L                 N
 P  L  A  Y  F  E  L  L  O  W
 A     E     E     M     A     D
 U  N  B  O  L  T     E  C  L  A  I  R
 K     M     A     L     A
 P  E  N  A  L     A  N  D  O  R  R  A
 T     N           S     W           Y
```

18

```
 P  I  R  A  C  Y     S  W  I  T  C  H
 E     E     R        A     R     U
 B  U  D  G  E     P  O  S  T  E  R  N
 B     W     T     A     H     N     G
 L  O  O  S  E  L  Y     O  R  D  E  R  Y
 E     O           M     U           Y
       D  E  S  C  A  R  T  E  S     S
 S           E     S           U     G
 T  W  A  N  G     T  E  M  P  L  A  R
 A     N     M     E     O     K     I
 B  U  G  B  E  A  R     T  R  I  A  L
 L     E     N           O     N     L
 E  R  R  A  T  A     B  R  O  G  U  E
```

19

```
       S  C     E     M
 J  A  C  K  A  N  D  J  I  L  L
 O     A     N     I     L     L
 L  I  M  B     N  I  C  K  L  E  B  Y
 N     I     T     T     I     O
 S  T  U  M  B  L  E     S  N  O  U  T
 H     A     Y     B     E     R
 H  E  A  D  Y     O  L  D  R  O  P  E
 C     R     L     O           A
 C  L  A  I  M  A  N  T     M  A  R  K
 U     G     N     C     O     T
    B  L  A  C  K  C  H  E  R  R  Y
       L     Y     Y     E
```

20

```
       S  F     S  C
    A  P  P  L  E  T  A  R  T
    T  A     I     R     O  P
 Z  I  N  C     G  O  O  D  W  O  R  K
    G     I     H     L     E
 T  H  R  O  A  T     L  A  T  E  S  T
    T     U           E     S
 P  R  I  S  O  N     C  H  A  N  G  E
    O     O           U     P     A
 O  P  E  R  A  T  O  R     A  R  N  O
    E     O     I     A     R     G
    F  A  V  O  U  R  I  T  E
       M     N     E     Y
```

21

22

23

24

25

```
M O U N T P L E A S A N T
I   S   O   A   D   S   O
S H E   P O U N D   S K I
O   L   N   E       L
O Z O N E   C O R A C L E
N   C   S   H       E   T
C R E A S E   P R O U S T
E   A       T   E   T   R
P A N C A K E   G H A N A
T   W   N   A       I
I D A   F I N A L   B U N
O   S   U   I   A   E
N O H O L D S B A R R E D
```

26

```
  C   T   A       W   T
T H I R D L Y   S H A W L
  I   U   T       I   O
O L D M A I D   S T A F F
  L   P   M   M   M   O
      S E V E R A L L Y
V   I   T   R   N   D
P A L M B E A C H
  N   P   R   E   S   G
W I E L D   K N U C K L E
  L   O       A   O   A
C L E R K   T R A P E Z E
  A   E       Y   E   E
```

27

```
O A T H S   S A P I E N T
P   O   H O P   A   M   O
T I A R A   Y A S H M A K
I   S   M       S   E   E
M O T H E R S H I P T O N
A   I   T   I   O       W
L I E   H E R O N   U L M
  L   E   E   F   P   A
B L I N D I N G L I G H T
U   R   E       O   R   I
G R I E V E D   W E A R S
L   S   I   O D E   D   S
E C H E L O N   R E E V E
```

28

```
  C H A F I N G D I S H
T   O   O   U   Y   T   S
R I G B Y   M E N   A A H
O   E   B   A   I   E
U P S U R G E   S I N G E
B   I       R   T       P
L O R D L Y   C Y P R U S
E   O   T       U   H
S W I N G   A N T O N I A
O   M   I   T   I       N
M O B   C O T   T R A C K
E   U   A   O   A   I   S
  B E L L F O U N D R Y
```

SOLUTIONS

29

```
A . S . K . M . S W A R M
P O P I N J A Y . O . E .
P . I . O . R . M O U S E
L U K E W A R M . L . I .
E . E . N . O . A S I D E
. D . A . T W O . A . U .
J U N G L E . A C C R U E
T . I . A R K . K . M .
A C U T E . A . V . B . B
. H . A . O F F I C I A L
E M P T Y . F . E . S . A
A . O . S L O W W O R M .
S N A R E . E . S . N . E
```

30

```
F I S T . S L U G G A R D
E . A . . . O . L . C . U
R I L L . S T R A W H A T
O . U . P . . . S . E . Y
C U T T L E F I S H . . .
I . A . A . L . C . I . C
T A R . T R I L L . M I R U
Y . Y . E . N . O . P . U
. . . F L I G H T L E S S
U . I . A . . H . R . A
S A V O Y A R D . M I N D
E . E . E . U . . A . E
D I S C R E E T . P L U S
```

31

```
. W . C . M . S . W
. H A R V E S T M O U S E
. I . A . T . A . M . I
S T I T C H . B U B B L E
. E . E . A . . . A . V
A F F R O N T . S T E E D
. E . . . E . T . . . R
M A R S H . F R A G I L E
. T . T . A . A . I
T H R U S H . M A R I N E
. E . F . U . W . . . I
P R O F I T M A R G I N
. . . Y . U . Y . . . G
```

32

```
. S U P P L E M E N T
F . U . O . I . E . E
L E G H O R N . L O R D S
A . A . L . N . O . V . I
S U R E . H E A D R O O M
H . . D . T . I . U . P
P U C K E R . W E A S E L
O . A . S . M . S . . . I
I N S P I R E D . C H I C
N . C . G . R . A . U . I
T R A I N . C A B A R E T
. D . E . I . E . O . Y
B E E R G A R D E N
```

33

```
N E P O T I S M   A G O G
O   O   A   E   T   R   O
R E L A X   D E W F A L L
M   E   C   A   E   S   D
  I M M O R T A L I S E D
S   I   L   E   F     U
C O C K L E   S T U B B S
A       E   T   H   L   T
F R E N C H W I N D O W
F   X   T   I   S   H
O U T P O S T   G U S T Y
L   O   R   C   H   O   M
D O L E   W H I T E M A N
```

34

```
S C R U M   R O S E T T E
A   I   O   E   E   H   N
R E F U S A L   D R E A D
A   L   E   A   A   M   E
C R E E L   T A N K A R D
E   E   L   I   G
N O T B E F O R E T I M E
    E   N   X       X
E R A S M U S   C L A M P
N   R   A   H   I   L   E
D R O W N   I N T R A I N
U   O   G   P   E   M   S
P O M P O U S   D R O V E
```

35

```
    F   G   A   S
  P O L T E R G E I S T
  L   A   R   A   N   R
Q U I P   B R I C K B A T
  M   I   N   U   F
S P Y H O L E   S N U F F
U   A   S   H   I   I
A D O R N   M Y S T I C S
D   D   G   P       A
P I S S A R R O   D A T A
N   H   A   N   E   O
  G R I Z Z L Y B E A R
    P   E   M   R
```

36

```
  O L D M A N R I V E R
B   E   I   A   L   M   G
A W A R D   S O L D I E R
L   T   S   S   U   L   E
M A H A T M A   S T Y L E
Y   E       U   E       N
  T R I C K   E D I F Y
S   O   H       L   S
P E P Y S   E N C H A N T
E   A   T   L   A   P   A
C A P T U R E   R E P E L
K   E   M   N   G   E   E
  F R E E M A S O N R Y
```

37

38

39

40

41

42

43

44

45

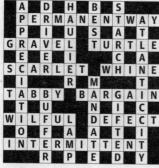

46

47

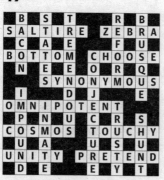

48

49

50

51

52

53

54

55

56

57

T	U	L	I	P		U	N	S	C	R	E	W
I		U		A		N		H		E		I
P	A	P	Y	R	U	S		R	A	D	O	N
S		I		S		E		E		R		C
T	E	N	O	N		N	O	W	H	E	R	E
E				I		T		S				
R	E	C	E	P	T	I	O	N	I	S	T	S
		O		M		I		I				C
P	E	R	V	A	D	E		T	E	M	P	O
A		D		R		N		R		O		U
N	O	I	S	Y		T	R	A	I	T	O	R
I		A		A		A		T		T		G
C	O	L	O	N	E	L		E	R	O	D	E

58

	R		S		P				P		S	
S	H	A	C	K	L	E		M	O	L	A	R
Y		H		A				I		V		
I	M	P	O	R	T		F	A	R	R	O	W
E		O		I		O		O		U		
			L	I	T	E	R	A	T	U	R	E
F			U		E					Y		
P	R	O	C	E	D	U	R	A	L			
E		H		E		U		O		S		
S	T	R	E	S	S		N	I	C	E	T	Y
S		R				N		K		A		
B	A	S	R	A		D	E	F	E	N	C	E
W		Y				R		T		K		

59

W	I	G	W	A	M		S	P	I	G	O	T
A		R		P			O		L			R
F	L	A	I	R		M	A	S	S	I	V	E
E		M		I		I		T		N		N
R	U	M	B	L	E	D		A	T	T	I	C
S		A		D		G						H
		R	E	P	E	L	L	E	N	T		
S		Y		E		E		O				S
T	O	P	E	R		S	Y	M	P	T	O	M
I		L		A		E		A		A		O
F	L	U	M	M	O	X		K	U	L	A	K
L		M		U		E		E		L		E
E	X	P	O	S	E		P	R	A	Y	E	R

60

		N		I		H		S				
	G	R	E	E	N	M	A	N	T	L	E	
	R		C		S		I		U		X	
B	E	A	K		T	I	T	I	C	A	C	A
A			E		I		K		L		
I	S	O	T	O	P	E		S	P	O	U	T
E		R		S		S		I			S	
S	P	O	O	K		C	H	A	G	R	I	N
R		U		B		R					V	
S	O	M	B	R	E	R	O		G	L	E	N
O		L		G		U		R		L		
F	R	E	E	A	N	D	E	A	S	Y		
		D		N		S		B				

61

62

63

64

65

66

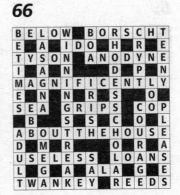

67

68

69

```
 P O T T I N G S H E D
O   I   E   A   H   N   H
V U L G A R I S E   T A O
E     C   L   E     R   R
R A J A H   E S T E E M S
B   A   E   D     C   E
E N C O R E   H U M O U R
A   Q   P   N   T   A
R O U N D E R   C R E E D
I   E   E   I   L     D
N O T   P O N D E R O U S
G   T   O   C   A   I   H
 R A T T L E S N A K E
```

70

```
  S   A   C   G   S
  O F F T H E R E C O R D
  U   L   A   I   O   I
U T M O S T   D E T E S T
  H   A   T       C   E
S P O T T E D   W H E A T
  A     R   S       N
S C O W L   S U B S I D E
  I   H   N   A   S
A F R E S H   D E L P H I
  I   R   E   O   O   I
S C A R L E T W O M A N
  Y   D   N   E   E
```

71

```
  P A P E R C H A S E
W   E   E   O   O   I
O L D H A N D   N I Z A M
O   A   T   E   D   A   A
D O L T   E N C U M B E R
P   F   T   R   L   I
E G G N O G   V A R E S E
C   U   R   B   S     L
K I N G S L E Y   I D O L
E   F   O   A   T   R   O
R H I N O   C H A R I T Y
    R   T   O   L   L   D
  M E C H A N I C A L
```

72

```
  P   A   P       B   V
G R A N A R Y   C O R A L
  I   I   O       T   R
D O O M E D   O B T A I N
  R   A   I   U   O   E
    L E G I T I M A T E
  W       I   S       Y
H A L L P O R T E R
  R   E   U   R   U   W
B R U G E S   E N D E A R
  I   A       T   D   U
F O R C E   A C R E A G E
  R   Y       H   R   H
```

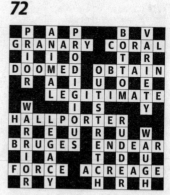

170

73

74

75

76

77

78

79

80

81

82

83

84

85

86

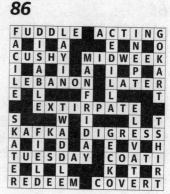

87

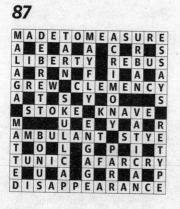

88

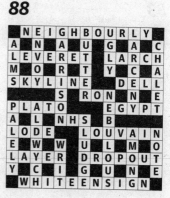

89

```
T R A N C E █ P L A C I D
U █ N █ U █ M █ E █ A █ I
M A Z U R K A █ P A R I S
B █ A █ T █ R █ E █ R █ N
L U C I A █ S A R D I N E
E █ I █ H █ █ █ E █ Y █ █
█ P R E L I M I N A R Y █
E █ E █ A █ E █ █ █ █ █ D
D I G I T A L █ C O P S E
I █ R █ U █ L █ K █ L █ N
T R E A D █ O U T L A S T
O █ S █ O █ W █ I █ I █ A
R O S A R Y █ F E N N E L
```

90

```
█ F A I N T H E A R T E D
G █ U █ E █ E █ L █ O █ I
R E C U R █ I S L A N D S
A █ T █ O █ G █ S █ A █ A
S H I N █ S H O W A L E G
S █ O █ G █ T █ E █ █ █ R
W A N T O N █ E L A P S E
I █ █ L █ U █ L █ U █ █ E
D I V I D E N D █ T R I M
O █ I █ F █ W █ T █ L █ E
W O R R I E R █ O N I O N
E █ U █ S █ A █ R █ E █ T
R O S E H I P S Y R U P █
```

91

```
C H A R A C T E R I S E D
L █ R █ S █ A █ E █ O █ O
E A T █ P L U G S █ B R A
A █ █ E █ G █ I █ █ █ S
R O V E R █ H O N E S T Y
T █ E █ S █ T █ W █ O █
H O R S E Y █ B U R E A U
E █ G █ █ P █ N █ E █ P
D R E S S E R █ L A P E L
E █ █ I █ O █ A █ █ █ E
C U B █ D I V O T █ G O A
K █ O █ L █ E █ C █ O █ S
S I X T E E N T H H O L E
```

92

```
█ B █ S █ B █ █ █ L █ B
T R I N K E T █ J I H A D
O █ I █ L █ █ █ M █ T █
H A P P I L Y █ A P T T O
█ D █ E █ I █ L █ E █ E
█ █ █ S C R I P T U R E
█ P █ S █ O █ B █ S █ Y
C O M P O S U R E █ █ █
█ R █ O █ E █ A █ A █ F
S T O R K █ D R I Z Z L E
█ I █ R █ █ █ I █ U █ O
E C L A T █ F A I R W A Y
█ O █ N █ █ █ N █ E █ T
```

93

```
C H A O S   P A R A S O L
O   C   A L E   E   O   A
O C A R O L   P L A Y L E T
K   O   A     D   I   T
S O B E R A S A J U D G E
H   A   I   H U   U
Y E T   E V E N S   W Y E
    L   D   E   T   I   A
M I L E S A N D M I L E S
E   Y   T     E   D   T
D O R M A N T   N I C H E
A   I   F   O U T   A   R
L U C I F E R   S A T A N
```

94

```
  A I D E M E M O I R E
S   S   P   S   L   E   I
H A M F I S T E D   P U N
E       S   A   I   U   T
P A T I O   T R E A D L E
H   R   D   E   I   R
E L E V E N   E M B A L M
R   A   E   A   T   I
D I T C H E S   C L E A N
E   M   A   P   B       G
S U E   U N I S E X U A L
S   N   N   E   T   F   E
  S T A T E S C H O O L
```

95

```
S   A   S   T   S M O C K
L I V E W I R E   A   R
O   A   I   E   S N E E R
P O S T P O N E   G   A
S   T   E D   F R O T H
  S   S   B S E   O   U
K E T T L E   L I V E R Y
  M   U   D R Y   E   E
B E R R Y   O   T O   I
  S   G   A B S O L V E D
S T E E L   E   O   I   L
  E   O   P R E T E N C E
F R O N T   T   H   E   R
```

96

```
S O C K   C A R B O L I C
H   O   P   I   I   I   A
R I L E   U P H O L D E R
E   O   P   E   C   O   P
W I S H Y W A S H Y
I   S   T   L   E   I   C
S O U G H T   A M A N D A
H   S   A   T   I   S   N
    A G G R E S S I O N
L   S   O   I   T   G   N
A S P I R A T E   K N O B
S   A   A   O   I   I   A
S I N G S I N G   B A W L
```

97

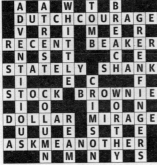

98

99

100

101

102

103

104

105

```
C O M P A S S I O N A T E
O   A   R   P   X   R   L
F O R S T E R   B L I M P
F   T   Y   U   R   E   A
E D I T   W C F I E L D S
E   A   F   E   D     O
  B L O O M   A G R E E
A   R   S   E   N   S
P A T I E N C E   S H O P
A   H   B   Y   L   A   I
C U R V E   L E A R N E R
H   O   A   L   W   C   I
E M B A R R A S S M E N T
```

106

```
  C O L D S T O R A G E
B   U   O   O   I   A   L
A T T E M P T   S A B L E
S   E   I   T   K   R   E
S Y R I N G E     V I E W
      A   R I G   E   A
B A C O N     R A L L Y
E   H   T A P   A
H E A T     H U N D R E D
A   R   L   Y   D   E   O
V A G U E   S T E R N U M
E   E   E   I   U   A   E
  D R E S S C I R C L E
```

107

```
U N S Y M P A T H E T I C
S   E   O   R   A   O   O
E K E   N O T E D   W A S
D   O   I   E   T
C U B I C   S I S T E R S
A   R   L   T   X   T
R A I D E R   C A L I P H
D   N   A   R   S   E
E N G A G E D   B A T H E
A   A   V   I   A
L O W   B L E A T   F A R
E   I   L   R   E   L   T
R O T T E N B O R O U G H
```

108

```
  B   A   U     E   C
E Y E B A L L   E N S U E
R   I   S     G   S
C O L D I T Z   S L O T H
N   E   E   F   I   O
      B R O A D S I D E
  C   A   M   R   H   Y
P R O G R A M M E
U   E   N   Y   C   T
S M I L E   H A I R I E R
P   E     R   O   N
F L A S K   E D I F I C E
E   S     S   T   H
```

109

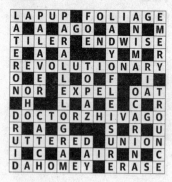

110

111

112

113

V	A	L	I	D	I	T	Y		I	C	O	N
A		A		I		A		S		A		O
M	I	N	U	S		S	O	L	O	M	O	N
P		G		O		M		E		E		S
	C	U	P	B	O	A	R	D	L	O	V	E
W		O		E		N		G		N		
A	B	R	A	D	E		G	E	N	I	U	S
T		I		C		H		L		E		
C	O	N	G	E	N	I	T	A	L	L	Y	
H		O		N		N		M		C		A
D	E	B	A	C	L	E		M	E	L	O	N
O		B		E		M		E		A		O
G	O	Y	A		H	A	R	R	I	D	A	N

114

P	U	L	L		S	C	O	T	S	M	A	N
A		E		S	U		I		A		O	
C	A	M	P	H	O	R		R	A	R	E	R
I		O		R		T		E		I		E
F	O	N	D	A		A	D	D	I	N	G	
I			N		I			E			B	
S	T	A	L	K	I	N	G	H	O	R	S	E
T		Q			R		A				D	
	T	U	N	D	R	A		G	O	A	T	S
S		A		R		I		G		W		T
N	I	T	R	E		S	A	L	V	A	G	E
A		I		A		E		E		K		A
P	O	C	K	M	A	R	K		S	E	N	D

115

	G		Z		C			S		E	
A	L	C	O	P	O	P		O	P	E	R	A
	O		D		N			O		A	
T	A	R	I	F	F		F	E	T	I	S	H
	T		A		L		A		T		U	
		C	H	U	R	C	H	Y	A	R	D	
H			E		E		E				E	
P	E	E	P	I	N	G	T	O	M		
R		O		C		O		I		L	
S	O	U	R	C	E		F	O	D	D	E	R
I		T			A		D		A		
P	S	A	L	M		O	C	U	L	I	S	T
M		Y			E		E		H		

116

B	U	S	T	L	E		S	W	E	D	E	N
I		A		A		R		R		O	
G	A	M	U	T		J	E	A	L	O	U	S
A		P		C		O		N		N		I
M	A	L	T	H	U	S		G	R	E	E	D
Y		E			S		L				E	
		R	E	P	O	S	S	E	S	S		
A			I		T			E			W	
N	O	T	E	S		I	M	P	U	L	S	E
T		I		T		C		U		F		A
H	A	D	D	O	C	K		T	H	I	N	K
E		A		L			T		S		E	
M	O	L	E	S	T		H	Y	P	H	E	N

117

118

```
O F I C
AVALANCHE
D E U B A S
PIER TURNPIKE
S W E E I
ACCORD DECENT
O R E F
BURKAS MARBLE
R U A E I
ISTANBUL MONK
E L T I O T
APPLICANT
S Y E Y
```

```
FORCEDLANDING
I E S A O R R
GALLANT WEAVE
U A U V A T B
RITE BIRDSEYE
E E F A A S
IDYLL KYOTO
T A S S U C
HOROWITZ INCH
O E L A A I O
UKASE TABASCO
G L S I L I S
HOMESECRETARY
```

119

120

121

122

123

124

125

126

127

128

129

```
  E S C A P O L O G Y
S D A   I   I A
O N W A R D S   T A L E S
U   I   T   T E   L O
T A N G   D O O R B E L L
H   D   N   A R   L I
B Y F O O T   F R A Y E D
O   A   M   H Y   A
U N C L E T O M   T H O R
N   T   S   T A   O I
D A U N T   D I S T A N T
A   I   O   I   R   Y
  B L A C K G U A R D
```

130

```
P O R P O I S E   C R A B
A   E   M   E S   E A
R A V E N   C A P T I O N
K   E   I   U R   G A
  P R O P O R T I O N A L
S   S   R   E N   I
T E E T E R   A G H A S T
O       S P   O V   Y
C O N S E Q U E N C E S
K   O   N   R I   N S
I N D I C E S   O U G H T
N   E   E   U N   E U
G I S T   M E A S U R E D
```

131

```
T O S S   S E N S I B L E
I   T   B X   E   A A
T R A D E U P   V E N U S
I   L   A E   E D   T
V A L E T   C O R R A L
A   I   T   G   A
T R U E T O O N E S E L F
E   N   R   A       F
  G L O R I A   R E V U E
I   O   O T   T   I C
B E V V Y   I N H E R I T
I   E   A   O Y   A E
S I D E L I N E   C L O D
```

132

```
  C   C   N     M   M
S H E L T E R   T A M A R
  A   E   W     S   J
G R A V E S   P I C K E T
  T   E   C   R   O   S
    R E A L E S T A T E
  T       S   V       Y
P R O P I T I A T E
O   O   E   L   X     P
F O W L E R   E X P E R T
P   I       N   A     I
K E A T S   S C A N D A L
R   E       E   D     M
```

133

```
    D P H V
  S O D A W A T E R
  C G D Z R R R
M A R S   D E A D B E A T
  T B E R     I
S H R O U D   D E B U N K
  A D       A G
A R G Y L E   S Y R I A N
  S S   N E O U
D I A M E T E R   N I G H
  S E   I A E E
    M A R C H P A S T
    L E H S
```

134

```
F L A S H I N T H E P A N
A L E O   O U   E
B O L L A R D   M I N O S
I S D   U E I   T
A L T O   C L E R I C A L
N A D   E U   E
  O R B I T   G L A S S
T   S A   E L   G
H E S I T A T E   Y O Y O
E E R O P B O
M A N I A   M A I L B A G
E S C I L E L
S P E C T A C U L A R L Y
```

135

```
  C O M P A R A T I V E
S S I A E I
H A I R N E T   L E T O N
O E E H L E G
E A R A C H E     U R G E
      O R E B A A
W O M A N       I N N E R
A E E R G D
F A M E     R A D I C A L
F E F U A R I
L O N E R   D U B I O U S
E T E G L U T
  C O N T R E T E M P S
```

136

```
B A T T L E   H E L M E T
I A E C I E I
S K I N N E R   D O M E D
H N I I E P D
O U T R E   M A R S H A L
P N I I Y
  W R I T I N G D E S K
D E A O S
W A G T A I L   G R O W L
I I C I S U U
G U M B O   T E T A N U S
H E R Y A C H
T E N A N T   G R E E D Y
```

137

```
  S C R I P T W R I T E R
I   O   O   A   E   B   E
N O N E T   P I T E O U S
D   S   A   P   A   N   E
I R O N   H E A R H E A R
A   R   O   D   D   R   V
N O T I C E   B E E T L E
A   T   R   D   R   D
P A S S A G E S   C A D S
O   I   V   P   A M   E
L A T T I C E   M A M B A
I   A   A   A   A   E   T
S T R A N G L E H O L D
```

138

```
C O L D C O L L A T I O N
O   B   O   A   S   M   O
N E W   C I V E T   F U R
S   K   I   E       T
E A S E L   S C R A T C H
Q   P   E   H       R   A
U N R E S T   O R D E A L
E   A   P   E   N   L
N A T U R A L   T I T L E
T   E   A   U       E   R
I O U   A U G E R   W E T
A   K   C   U   N   O   O
L I E C H T E N S T E I N
```

139

```
  M   S   T       C   F
V E N T U R E   S H O R T
  R   U   A       E   A
B R O C A D E   F R O N D
  Y   K   I   M   I   T
          S T E A M S H I P
  H   S   I   R   H   C
P A C K H O R S E
  R   I   N   U   B   C
S M I T E   S P A R T A N
  O   T   I   O   I
A N K L E   W A R T O R N
  Y   E   L   H   O
```

140

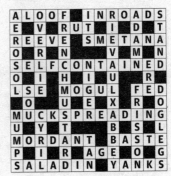

```
A L O O F   I N R O A D S
E   V   R U T   I   D   T
R E E V E   S M E T A N A
O   R   N   V   M   N   N
S E L F C O N T A I N E D
O   I   H   I   U   R
L S E   M O G U L   F E D
  O   U   E   X   R   O
M U C K S P R E A D I N G
U   Y   T       B   S   L
M O R D A N T   B A S T E
P   I   R   A G E   O   G
S A L A D I N   Y A N K S
```

141

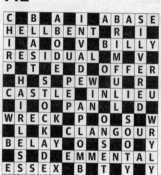

142

143

144

145

```
  F L U I D O U N C E
T   I   N   A   N   A
H O L Y D A Y   B U R N T
O   E   O   B   U   P   H
R A T E   N E X T D O O R
O       P   D   T   R   E
U N S H O D   R O S T R A
G   I   L   H   N       D
H A N D Y M A N   C H U B
L   E   G   R   O   A   A
Y O D E L   R E M O T E R
    I   O   O   I   C   E
  D E A T H W A T C H
```

146

```
C O M E B A C K   A M O K
U   I   L   U   L   A   I
F E N C E   S O U L F U L
F   A   E   T   M   I   K
  P R I D E O F P L A C E
A   E   T   M   S       N
L O T I O N   P O I S O N
S   S   D   O   F   T   Y
A S H W E D N E S D A Y
T   O   A   E   U   M   M
I M P U T E D   G Y P S Y
A   E   H   G   A   O   T
N A S H   R E T R E N C H
```

147

```
P U S H   I C E C R E A M
O   H   G   O   L   X   U
U N I C O R N   A S P I C
L   R   D   T   I   O   H
T U T T I   R U M O U R
I   V   A       N   N   C
C U S T A R D P O W D E R
E   T   I   C       U   U
  P A R S E C   C H E S S
T   N   P   T   U   Y   A
R A D I I   I L L B R E D
E   B   R   O   T   I   E
K E Y S T O N E   V E E R
```

148

```
  B   H   A     S   C
H O M E R U N   V E N O M
  E   R   T     R   N
B R O O C H   W H I M S Y
  S   I   O   A   E   I
      C U R A T E S E G G
  D   S   E       N
P E R I P H E R A L
  L   N   I   S   E   W
M I S H A P   P A T C H Y
  G   E   O   T       A
S H A R K   Q U I E T L Y
  T   E   T   R   E
```

149

H	A	M	M	E	R		A	B	O	U	N	D
O		E		R			R		N			E
M	I	A	O	U		S	T	A	T	I	S	M
A		S		P		E		N		T		I
G	A	L	A	T	E	A		T	R	E	S	S
E		E		S		S		U				E
		S	C	H	O	O	L	B	O	Y		
G			I		N			A		F		
R	E	S	I	T		I	N	V	E	R	S	E
O		C		C		N		I	D			I
W	A	R	T	H	O	G		G	N	A	T	S
T		A		I		I		R				T
H	U	M	A	N	E		B	L	I	M	E	Y

150